# The War Is Real

By
Vaughn Allen

**TEACH Services, Inc.**
Brushton, New York

## Facsimile Reproduction

As this book played a formative role in the development of Christian thought and the publisher feels that this book, with its candor and depth, still holds significance for the church today. Therefore the publisher has chosen to reproduce this historical classic from an original copy. Frequent variations in the quality of the print are unavoidable due to the condition of the original. Thus the print may look darker or lighter or appear to be missing detail, more in some places than in others.

2010  11  12  13  14  ·  5  4  3  2  1

Copyright © 2004 TEACH Services, Inc.
ISBN-13: 978-1-57258-269-9
Library of Congress Control Number: 2004100755

Published by

**TEACH Services, Inc.**
*www.TEACHServices.com*

# Contents

# Abbreviations of Sources

# Acknowledgments

It is appropriate that I acknowledge my indebtedness to several persons without whose cooperation this book could never have been written.

To my wife I am indebted for her sympathetic understanding, for her willingness to spend many hours alone while I was writing this book and while I was engaged in spiritual warfare, and for joining me at times in these spiritual battles.

To all with whom it has been my privilege to engage in spiritual warfare, some of whose experiences are recorded on these pages, I am deeply indebted although for the sake of their privacy they must remain anonymous.

To Julie Snyder, who kindly and efficiently typed the manuscript, I am much indebted.

But more than to anyone else, I am indebted to Jesus Christ who, as Commander in Chief of the loyal angelic army, is even now doing battle on behalf of each one of us.

That battle indeed is real. But because of Him, so is the victory!

# Introduction

Clever book titles abound, often obscuring the real message of the author. Not this one. This book discusses exactly what its title announces: the reality of the spiritual warfare daily facing God's people and the certainty of victory!

Few Christians grasp the vast implications of this awesome and wonderful truth. Most of us have understood correctly that the great controversy between Christ and Satan is a megastruggle of enormous theological and historical significance. This galactic battle between the forces of good and evil is being played out in grand scale before a watching universe right here on planet Earth. And though the struggle is fierce and grows in intensity as the conflict nears its climax, victory, because of our Saviour's triumph on Calvary's battlefield, is guaranteed.

But many of us do not comprehend fully, I suspect, that there is a micro version of this warfare that goes on every second of every day and that we personally stand front and center as the principal combatant-actors on this cosmic stage.

The two extremes to be avoided, as C. S. Lewis has wisely cautioned, are the outright denial of Satan's existence and activity in our world today, and an obsessive preoccupation with him and his work—the devil-behind-every-bush mentality.

Tragically, many of us today have slipped into a third attitude toward the enemy that carries equal if not greater consequences than the first two—the ostrich outlook. Too many are burying their heads in the sand, refusing to look at or recognize the enemy's strategies and devices. Inspired counsel tells us that by neglecting to learn Satan's tactics, we give him an almost "inconceivable advantage,"[1] and that he could not gain the advantage over us which he so often does if we had a better understanding of his methods of attack.[2] It is my belief that reading this book carefully and prayerfully will go a long way toward giving you, the reader, that "better understanding."

The material contained on the following pages is biblical and solidly supported from the voluminous supplemental inspiration graciously given our people in the spirit of prophecy. It is an exposé of the enemy's most successful strategies against the people of God, and at the same time, it reveals the nature of our spiritual weapons—offensive and defensive[3]—which God graciously supplies to thwart Satan and route his forces.

Satan, more than anyone else, knows all about our peculiar potency under God, that once we understand this great truth of our position and authority in Christ (and apply it), his power over us is broken. The possibility that God's people will come to this vital understanding causes Satan and his evil troops to tremble, for they know that the believer's power in Christ is not like a stray shot across the bow, but more like a thirty-megaton warhead fired down the smokestack! This is why the enemy of souls must at all costs keep us blinded to this spiritual reality.[4] He can't risk a Pentecost II!

If there is such a thing as a "secret weapon" in the great controversy, the special insights elaborated on in these pages could very well be it. Read this book reflectively and prayerfully—you may never be the same again.

—Dr. George H. Akers

---

1. GC 516
2. 1 T 308
3. 2 Corinthians 10:1-5
4. 3 SM 423

# Chapter 1
# War in the Hospital

"My name is Seizure."

The words came from Donna's throat just seconds after I had begun to pray for her in the hospital room. That voice proved later to be only the first of more than sixty such voices who spoke through Donna's vocal chords and who identified themselves during the next few hours as I continued to pray for her healing.

"I won't go! I won't go!"

For a minute or so, the voice continued to protest its having to leave. But soon, after one final loud scream, Donna's body relaxed and the voice became quiet.

Donna was a young woman who had been admitted to an Adventist medical center several days earlier because she was experiencing increasingly frequent and severe seizures. Because of some of the things which transpired later, I must tell you that Donna was an unusually attractive young woman. She was twenty-one years of age.

During her stay in the hospital, a day or two before I met her, several unusual things happened to Donna which were witnessed by some of the nurses and other hospital staff. On one occasion Donna was picked up by unseen hands and thrown against the wall, causing a large "goose egg" to appear on her head. Another time she was literally thrown down a flight of stairs in the hospital. Though uninjured, she became so violent it required six nurses and orderlies to get her back into her bed and put restraints on her. She broke the restraints almost immediately, seemingly with little effort.

The physician in charge of the department told Donna's parents that he could not diagnose Donna's type of seizure and that it was "too deep" for them to treat. It was then that Donna's parents contacted me and asked me to come to the hospital and pray for their daughter.

I met Donna's parents and her older sister around nine o'clock on a Saturday evening in one of the hospital's waiting rooms. I learned that Donna was basically an Adventist Christian, but had recently become careless in her observance of the Sabbath and had developed quite an interest in rock music. She had experienced three recent bouts with pneumonia. And then the seizures had begun. The seizures became so frequent and severe that her parents admitted her to the hospital for examination and treatment. All this I learned as we walked down the corridor to Donna's room.

### Other Voices Spoke

A few minutes later, with Donna in her bed and surrounded by her family and friends, I began to pray on Donna's behalf. It was then that "Seizure," the first of more than sixty such voices, spoke from her.

Space does not permit me to discuss each of these voices, nor is it necessary to do so. But I do want to share with you our experience with three or four of the voices in order that you may realize the reality of the situation.

*"Sabbath-keeping."* *"My name is Sabbath-keeping,"* said one voice. *"My assignment is to keep Donna from observing the Sabbath."* I remembered then that Donna's parents had told me that she had become careless in regard to the Sabbath.

*"Medication."* Two doctors, one of whom was an intern, joined us in several sessions of prayer. During one of those prayer sessions, one of the voices said, *"My name is Medication. My work is to see that the doctors give her too much medicine."* Some time later as we were walking down the corridor during a break, the doctor said to me, "When you think of it, what are we doing but giving shots and pills and

other forms of medication?" (For the true effects of drugs, see 2SM 450-452.)

*"Pride."* During the entire experience, while we were praying, Donna was awake and alert. She knew what was going on. She prayed with us at times and carried on a conversation at other times; but her prayers and conversation were interrupted by the voices which spoke through her, but over which she had no control. One of the last voices to speak in this way identified himself as "Pride." As soon as the voice said, *"My name is Pride,"* Donna began to weep. Tears flowed from her eyes and down her cheeks.

"Oh, yes," she said, "I have been so proud." And then she began to pray. She prayed the same short prayer over and over for the next thirty minutes. I know because I timed it. I prayed silently as Donna's oral prayer was punctuated by the voice shouting, "I won't go! I don't want to go!" I heard Donna's prayer so often during that half hour and it so impressed itself on my mind that I can still repeat it word for word. She prayed:

"Oh, Lord, I have been so proud. Please forgive me. I've spent so much time in front of the mirror admiring my face, my figure, my hair, and my clothing. Please forgive me. From this time on, when I look into the mirror, let me see only the beauty of my Saviour."

As we both continued to pray, there was that final loud cry of protest that I had heard so often, and Donna's body relaxed and the voice was silent.

*"Game-playing."* Donna and I, with some of her family members, continued in almost constant prayer from Saturday evening until Monday noon. The last of the voices spoke a little before twelve o'clock on Monday. At about 11:30 Donna suddenly sat up in her bed and looked directly at me.

*"Pastor Allen, I want to apologize to you. You have been so kind. You have spent so many hours with me. I really appreciate it. And it's really all my fault. I am sorry and I apologize again. Please take your Bible and go home. I'm all right, really. Just take your Bible and go home. There aren't any demons here. I did this all myself just to get attention.*

*Now, take your Bible and go home."*

If this had been my first experience in dealing with demonic forces I might have been deceived, for the persuasive voice sounded very genuine. But this was not my first such experience. There was much evidence pointing to the fact that there *were* demons involved; indeed, that it was a demon who was even then speaking through Donna and urging me to take my Bible and go home.

"You are not Donna speaking," I said, looking straight into Donna's eyes. "You are a demon speaking through Donna. God knows that, you know that, and I know that. Donna has chosen to serve Jesus Christ, and you have no legal right to be in her or to use her vocal chords. In the name of Jesus Christ whom both Donna and I serve, I command that you tell me your name and that you leave."

*"My name is Game-playing,"* came the answer. Then, with the usual cry of protest coming from her throat, Donna relaxed and there were no more voices.

## "Exorcism," "Spiritual Battle," and "Deliverance"

Donna was discharged from the medical center about five o'clock that afternoon. In the words of one of her doctors, "They [the seizures] stopped immediately" after our prayer sessions which he calls "an exorcism."[1] I avoid using the term *exorcism* because I believe that the word has a negative connotation in the minds of many people. I prefer to think of such prayer as I engaged in for Donna as a "spiritual battle" which results in a "deliverance" involving the ministry of the Holy Spirit and the holy angels. These terms are more in harmony with my understanding of Scripture and the writings of Mrs. E. G. White.

However, whether we prefer the word *exorcism* or some other word having the same meaning, we must recognize that the doctor is suggesting that demons were present in Donna's body and that it was these superhuman forces who were speaking through her in that hospital room.

Could this possibly have been the case? Is it possible that in this enlightened, sophisticated, and scientific age, people—

even professing Christians—can be controlled or possessed by demonic powers? Can demons actually use the vocal chords of human beings and speak through them as they spoke through Donna?

To find the answers to these and related questions, we must turn to the Scriptures and to the writings of Mrs. E. G. White, for they are the only authoritative sources of information on this subject.

## The Great Controversy

The Bible plainly teaches that the planet on which we live is the scene of the most devastating conflict ever to occur anywhere in God's entire universe. We can understand all other teachings of the Bible only when we view them in the light of this controversy. We can find satisfactory answers to life's large questions only when we understand the nature, origin, purpose, and outcome of this conflict which is going on between the forces of Satan and the forces of Jesus Christ.

This concept of the great controversy—of its origin, its conduct, and its eventual outcome—is central to Seventh-day Adventist theology. More than any other single doctrine, the truth of this controversy with its many implications forms the backdrop of our beliefs. The great Bible truths which form "the pillars of our faith"[2]— the Sabbath truth, the true state of the dead, the sanctuary message, the second advent—are all inseparably associated with the controversy which is now going on and in which each of us is involved. Ultimately, when the conflict has ended, only two facts—that each of us is caught up in this war and that Jesus Christ has already won the victory—will be seen to have mattered in this life. Everything else—those things we give so much of our time and attention to now—will then be seen as having been subordinate.

*Origin of the conflict.* The Bible does not leave us in any doubt as to the origin of the controversy. It began in the most unlikely of all places—the perfect environment of heaven. This fact alone should tell us something about the subtle nature of sin. Sin is a mystery which cannot be excused, explained, or understood. Lucifer, a perfect being,[3] the highest of all angels, challenged God's government and maligned His character. The inspired record states the fact in simple terms: "There was war in heaven."[4] Lucifer (later called Satan) and all the angels who sympathized with him fought against Christ and the loyal angels. Eventually Satan "was cast out into the earth, and his angels were cast out with him." In this way our planet became the battlefield in the greatest war ever waged. It has remained a battlefield ever since. And it will continue to be the scene of conflict until Satan and his followers—both angelic and human—are destroyed, with only a brief interlude during the millennium.[5]

*The enemy.* Until we understand some things about Satan, who is the instigator and chief proponent of the rebellion, we cannot understand the significance of the controversy. Many Christians, including some Seventh-day Adventists, are afraid to talk or read about Satan. But his hatred and warfare will not be any less because we ignore him. In fact, nothing makes him happier or pleases him more than for us to pretend that he does not exist, or for us to think of him as having cleft hoofs, horns, a long tail, and pitchfork as he is often portrayed in cartoons. He is pleased when he is regarded as the object of a myth, when he is ignored or made light of. All of this suits his purpose well; it plays right into his plans.[6]

On the other hand, "there is nothing that the great deceiver fears so much as that we shall become acquainted with his devices."[7] "He [Satan] could not gain advantage if his methods of attack were understood."[8] And so it is my purpose in these pages to help us become acquainted with some of the enemy's devices—to expose some of his methods of attack—and to show how, through Christ, we can gain the victory. In doing this, I shall draw upon the Bible, the writings of Mrs. E. G. White, and my experience during the past ten years in ministering to those who, like Donna, have found themselves severely harassed, controlled, or possessed by the enemy.

*Not to extol the enemy.* It is true that we have been cautioned against thinking and talking too much about the enemy and his power.[9] We must not in any way extol him or overemphasize his influence. But we are also told that one reason we have so little enmity against him—so little ability to resist him—is that we are terribly ignorant concerning his power and hatred. We do not realize the vast extent of his warfare against Christ and the church.[10]

*Not to remain ignorant.* Since we *are* the church—the objects of the enemy's hatred—it behooves us to know all we can about the enemy, his plans, and his methods. Mrs. E. G. White tells us that "in the final crisis he [the enemy] will deceive to their own ruin those *who do not now seek to understand his methods of working.*"[11] She points out that among professed Christians, and even among ministers of the gospel, there is seldom heard any reference to Satan except in an incidental way. We find it very easy to ignore the many signs of his craftiness that are all around us. Of course Satan would be happy for us to remain in this ignorant condition because "his [Satan's] great success lies in keeping men's minds confused, and ignorant of his devices, for then he can lead the unwary as it were, blindfolded."[12]

*Extremes to be avoided.* There are two extremes, two errors, which must be avoided. The first error, as we have seen, is to doubt Satan's existence—to make light of him and downplay his power. The second error is just as dangerous, and that is to become preoccupied with him. It does not matter to the enemy whether we ignore him or become obsessed with him. Either to ignore him or to see him under every rock and behind every bush is to give him all the advantage he needs. Both extremes are to be avoided.

*Satan, the enemy.* The Bible leaves us no room to doubt or question who the enemy is in this conflict, for it plainly identifies him as "that old serpent, which is the Devil, and Satan."[13] Our enemy today is the same one who caused the downfall of our first parents in the Garden of Eden.[14] But Satan is not our only enemy, for fighting on his side and taking their orders from him are wicked spirits.[15] These are fallen angels whom we usually call demons.

**The Nature of the War**

It is not enough that we recognize the reality and power of

the *enemy*. We must also recognize the reality of the *war*. The personal, day-to-day battle is every bit as real as the enemy is. "It is not mimic battles in which we are engaged. We are waging a warfare upon which hang eternal results. We have unseen enemies to meet. Evil angels are striving for the dominion of every human being."[16]

In recent years most of us have become very aware of the dangers that threaten our property and our lives. Consequently, we resort to locks and alarm systems to protect ourselves. But because we cannot see them, we seldom think of the evil angels who are constantly seeking to harm us, and against whose attacks we have no natural defense. Yet, "if permitted, they [evil angels] can distract our minds, disorder and torment our bodies, destroy our possessions and our lives."[17]

**The War Is Most Severe Today**

The passing of time since Satan's expulsion from heaven has not diminished his hatred for God or lessened in the least his determination to destroy God's government and the entire human family. In fact, the opposite is true. With the passing of time, Satan, who knows his time is running out, has become more desperate; his anger—hotter; his methods—more subtle; and his attacks—more numerous. We can be sure that at this stage of the war, he is not going to abandon any device or method which he has found to be successful in the past. On the contrary, "every ingenious device will be used, every possible method taken advantage of."[18] For good reason does the Bible speak of Satan as "having great wrath, because he knoweth that he hath but a short time."[19]

*Satan's power has increased a hundredfold.* In the meantime, while the controversy continues, Satan's power to tempt and deceive is being sharpened and refined by constant practice. Consequently, his power is a hundred times greater today than it was when he rebelled,[20] and it will continue to increase with use until he is destroyed.[21] Satan's powers of persuasion, too, are almost beyond our human comprehension. So great are they that he persuaded one third of the angels of heaven to join him in his rebellion.[22] Right now Satan is using those same enticing powers of persuasion to deceive and trap us in his snares. So while we must remember that Jesus has "all power . . . in heaven and in earth" at His command[23] and that He has already won the victory, we must not underestimate Satan's ability to wage war and to charm and persuade. Satan will use his persuasive power at the close of the millennium to convince his angels and the wicked that they can actually capture the New Jerusalem.[24] And Jesus strongly implied that in the last days the enemy will come close to deceiving "the very elect."[25] Therefore it behooves each one of us to abide in Christ and be constantly on guard.

*The battle is more severe today than at any other time.* Because Satan becomes more desperate with each passing year, "the great controversy going on in the world is waging more sharply today than at any period of this world's history."[26] We may be tempted to think that the battle is less severe today than it was in the days of the Roman empire when Christian martyrs were thrown to the lions, or in the Middle Ages when many of God's faithful ones were called upon to give their lives at the stake. But that is not the case. It is only that the enemy has temporarily changed his tactics. Instead of persecution as his main tool, he now uses the more subtle tool of compromise to accomplish his purpose.

Through drugs, pornography, various forms of demonic music, witchcraft, Satan worship, and in a hundred other ways, Satan is cunningly gaining control of human minds. As a result, we are today witnessing mass murders, suicides, accidents, and other forms of violence on an unprecedented scale. We are amazed at the immorality in the world and at the lack of true piety in the church. The divorce rate in the church today is not far behind that of the world. Total abstinence from the use of alcohol and drugs is no longer the lifestyle of many Adventist young people, nor of some who are not so young. The battle lines are drawn. The controversy not only continues; it becomes more intense with each passing year.

*We are living on a battlefield,* and life on a battlefield is never pleasant. It means pain, suffering, destruction, and death. But it also means healing and gains and victories. Life on a battlefield consists of what we see going on around us in the world and in the church. Everywhere we look, we see conclusive evidence that we are living in the war zone.

## The War Is a Personal One

As a people, Adventists have always known that there is a controversy being fought between Christ and Satan. And we have known that the battle involves "the church." However, it has been easy for us to think of "the church" as a collective and impersonal term, and to forget that "the church" is people. The church is you and me. And it is on this personal level that battles are won or lost. While we may be aware of the controversy in its general nature, I suspect that few of us have begun to realize how personal the battles are, or to what extent we are individually involved. Neither do most of us recognize the severity of the battle or how subtle and crafty Satan's devices are. And as we shall see, he is quick to take advantage of our ignorance.

It is essential to our individual salvation and to the successful mission of the church that we be informed in regard to Satan's methods and devices. To remain ignorant is to invite spiritual defeat and eternal loss.

## We Have Supernatural Help

Not all the angels involved in the controversy are fallen. For every angel who joined Satan in his rebellion, there are two who remained loyal. These unfallen angels have an active and important part in the battle. If the curtain could be drawn back so that we could see the battle as it is actually being fought, we would see these loyal angels flying swiftly to help those who are tempted. We would see these angels, commissioned from heaven, actually forcing the evil angels to retreat. We would see that "the battles waging between the two armies are as real as those fought by the armies of this world, and on the issue of the spiritual conflict eternal destinies depend."[27]

Although this world is Christ's battlefield,[28] He has not deserted us to fight the enemy alone. Rather than leave even one soul to be overcome by Satan, He would empty heaven of every angle to come to the rescue.[29]

1. *Channels* (Fall 1986), published by It Is Written Telecast, 1100 Rancho Conejo Blvd., Newbury Park, CA 91320. Article by Dr. Clarence Carnahan, page 5.
2. 2SM 388, 389
3. Ezekiel 28:15
4. Revelation 12:7-9
5. Revelation 20:1-3, 7-10
6. 1T 342
7. GC 516
8. 1T 308
9. DA 493
10. GC 507
11. RH, July 16, 1901 (emphasis supplied)
12. 3SM 423
13. Revelation 20:2
14. Genesis 3:1-5, 14
15. Ephesians 6:12
16. MH 128
17. GC 517
18. TDWG 312
19. Revelation 12:12
20. 3T 328
21. 2SG 277
22. Revelation 12:4
23. Matthew 28:18
24. Revelation 20:7-9
25. Matthew 24:24
26. UL 20
27. MB 119
28. 4BC 1163
29. GC 560

# Chapter 2
# The War and the Gospel Commission

Both the earthly ministry of Jesus and His giving of the gospel commission at its close emphasize the reality and severity of the battle; and they also reveal the personal nature of the conflict.

### Jesus Met the Enemy Face to Face

Since Christ's purpose in coming to this earth was to defeat the enemy on his own ground, we can be sure He was actively involved in the war every waking hour of the thirty years He lived on the battlefield. His ministry is summarized in these words: "God anointed Jesus of Nazareth with the Holy Ghost and with power: who went about doing good, and healing all that were oppressed of the devil; for God was with him."[1]

The Bible records a number of instances in Christ's ministry where He came face to face with the enemy. Matthew tells of the experience of a man who was so controlled by Satan that he had lost his God-given ability to speak. "When the devil was cast out, the dumb spake: and the multitude marvelled, saying It was never so seen in Israel."[2]

The healing of the demon-possessed boy at the foot of the Mount of Transfiguration is a well-known experience in Christ's ministry.[3] The father's description of the boy's affliction in Mark 9:18, 20 seems to indicate that the boy was subject to some type of seizure. Whatever the problem was, it had begun when the victim was a child. The record says that Jesus addressed the demon, "Thou dumb and deaf spirit, I charge

21

thee, come out of him, and enter no more into him." In response to Christ's command, the demon cried out and convulsed the boy's body. But, as still happens today, he left in spite of his protests.

Possibly the best-known of all such healings is that of the demoniac of Gadara, recorded in Mark 5.[4] In this case Jesus, after commanding them to leave, addressed the demons who held the man prisoner, asking, "What is thy name?" The demon answered, "My name is Legion: for we are many." After the demons pleaded with the Saviour to send them into a herd of swine rather than out of the country, Jesus gave them leave. And as always, the demons obeyed.

All of these people, and the many others whom Jesus healed in a similar way, were prisoners of Satan. They had truly been taken captive by him. But early in His ministry Jesus had declared that He had come "to heal the brokenhearted, to preach deliverance to the captives, and . . . to set at liberty them that are bruised."[5] In harmony with His declared mission, Jesus set these people free by casting out the demonic powers that controlled them.

### Demons "Came Out"

Concerning the healings in Christ's ministry which involved the casting out of demons, Mrs. E. G. White points out that "in nearly every instance, Christ addressed the demon as an intelligent entity, commanding him to come out of his victim and to torment him no more."[6] The point she is making is this: Demons were real beings in Christ's day, and He recognized them as such. We, too, should realize that demons are real beings. This is why it is possible for them to speak through their victims and to identify themselves and their "work" or assignment in that particular victim, as they often do.

In most of these cases the demons are spoken of as "coming out" of their victims. They "came out" because they had been living "in" those whom they afflicted. The bodies of these human beings, intended by God to be the dwelling places of the Holy Spirit, had actually become the habitations of demons or fallen angels. Demonic powers had such control over the physical bodies of those people, that the demons literally possessed the senses, the nerves, the organs, and the emotions. The demons spoke through their victims, using the victims' vocal chords. It is important that we recognize these facts as part of the reality of the war.

Though the individual experiences are not recorded, the Bible indicates that there were many others whom Christ healed in this same way. "When even was come, they brought unto him many that were possessed with devils: and he cast out the spirits with his word, and healed all that were sick: that it might be fulfilled which was spoken by Esaias the prophet, saying, Himself took our infirmities, and bare our sicknesses."[7]

These people whom Jesus healed by casting out demons were not merely suffering from natural causes. Supernatural powers were at work, and Christ well understood what and whom He was dealing with. "He recognized the direct presence and agency of evil spirits."[8]

### Demons Inhabit Human Bodies Today

The fact that human bodies were inhabited by demons in Christ's day must be recognized by everyone who believes the New Testament record. But what about today? Can demons live in human bodies today as they did in Christ's time?

The honest answers to four simple questions should help us arrive at the right conclusion to this important question.

1. Is Satan "friendlier" now than he was in Christ's time?
2. Has Satan's *nature* changed since Christ was upon earth?
3. Has Satan's *purpose* changed since that time?
4. Since Satan is waging war more severely today than at any other time in history, is it logical to believe he would abandon any scheme or device which he had found successful in the past?

The answer to each of these question, of course, must be an emphatic No. Can demons inhabit and control human bodies even in our supposedly civilized and sophisticated culture of today? Of course they can. And they do—more often than most of us believe.

Satan and his demonic forces can distract our minds. They can disorder and torment our physical bodies. When they are permitted to do so, they can destroy our possessions just as they did in Job's case.[9] And when God allows it, they can destroy our lives.[10] "Satan's influence is constantly exerted upon men to distract the senses, control the mind for evil, and incite to violence and crime. He weakens the body, darkens the intellect, and debases the soul."[11]

If Satan cannot destroy us physically, he will attempt to destroy us spiritually, morally, or intellectually. The battle, we must remember, is "for real." "It is not mimic battles in which we are engaged,"[12] but they are "as real as those fought by the armies of the world."[13]

Since the stakes are so high, Satan will resort to any means at his command to accomplish his purpose. He will do anything he can to tempt, mislead, control, or possess us. He will find every opening and take advantage of every opportunity. He is bound by no principle except his own self-interest. This enemy who had power to take the Son of God in his arms and carry Him to a pinnacle of the temple will, if permitted, exercise the same power over you and me who are far inferior to Jesus, who are almost totally ignorant of his craftiness and strength, and who are already by nature inclined to do his bidding.[14] These are the grim realities of war.

### We Are to Continue Christ's Work

But our Saviour did not abandon us when He left this planet to return to heaven. He who knows our weaknesses and Satan's strengths did not leave us at the mercy of an enemy who knows no mercy. In giving the gospel commission, Jesus provided that His work should be carried on by His disciples and by His church. In a prayer to His Father just before He was arrested in the Garden of Gethsemane, Jesus said, "As thou has sent me into the world, even so have I also sent them [His disciples] into the world."[15]

Just as "God anointed Jesus of Nazareth with the Holy Ghost and with power: who went about doing good, and healing all that were oppressed of the devil,"[16] likewise Jesus "called unto him his twelve disciples, [and] he gave them power against unclean spirits, to cast them out, and to heal all manner of sickness and all manner of disease."[17]

Luke puts it this way: "He called his twelve disciples together, and gave them power and authority over all devils, and to cure disease."[18] Luke emphasizes the fact that the disciples were given "authority" as well as "power" over "all devils," without any exceptions.

Mark records the gospel commission in these significant words: "He said unto them, Go ye into all the world, and preach the gospel to every creature. He that believeth and is baptized shall be saved; but he that believeth not shall be damned." Then he states that certain signs will happen wherever the gospel is preached. And the first sign Mark gives is that wherever the gospel is preached, the disciples shall "cast out devils."[19]

After commenting on Mark's version of the gospel commission, Mrs. White points out that both the commission and the promises that accompany it are as valid today as when Jesus spoke them to His disciples. Then she asks, "Why should we not today witness the same results?"[20]

Perhaps the following two sentences from the same writer will help to answer the question; "I saw that if the church had always retained her peculiar, holy character, the power of the Holy Spirit which was imparted to the disciples would still be with her. The sick would be healed, devils would be rebuked and cast out, and she [the church] would be mighty and a terror to her enemies."[21]

Both the Bible and the writings of Mrs. White make it plain that in carrying out the gospel commission, the church is to do the very work which Christ did when He was on earth. We have already noticed that Jesus said He was sending His disciples into the world in the same way that His Father had sent Him into the world. Mrs. White makes the same point with these words: The followers of Christ are to labor as He did. "We are to feed the hungry, clothe the naked, and comfort the suffering and afflicted. . . . Through His servants, God designs that the sick, the unfortunate,

and *those possessed of evil spirits shall hear His voice.*
Through His human agencies He desires to be a comforter
such as the world knows not."[22]

These words should alert members of the remnant church
as to our God-given responsibilities and privileges in fulfilling
the gospel commission. We are to labor as He labored. We are
to apply ourselves to every phase of the ministry which Christ
carried on.[23]

## Satan Heard the Gospel Commission

When Christ gave the gospel commission to His disciples,
Satan heard it too, and recognized its significance. Because of
what he had heard, he called a meeting of all his angelic forces
soon after Christ's ascension. Satan admitted to them that he
had failed in defeating Christ while He was here on the battlefield. Satan told his demonic forces that from that time on,
they must bend all their efforts toward defeating Christ's followers. In every generation, they must seek to ensnare those
who believe in Him. Satan demanded of his fallen angels that
they work ten times harder against the church than they had
worked against Christ. Satan revealed to his evil spirits "that
Jesus had given His disciples power to rebuke them and cast
them out, and to heal those whom they should afflict. Then
Satan's angels went forth like roaring lions, seeking to destroy
the followers of Jesus."[24]

In harmony with Satan's orders, the work of the fallen angels is now "ten-fold greater than it was in the days of the
apostles. His power has increased, and it will increase, until it
is taken away. His wrath and hate grow stronger as his time
to work draws near its close."[25]

## We Are Still in the Same War

We who make up the remnant church today are bound by
the gospel commission just as surely as were the original disciples and the early Christian church. The war is not over. We
live today on the same battlefield where Jesus lived. We face
the same enemy He and His disciples faced. The main thrust
of the commission is to "preach the gospel," but the battle

must be fought on all fronts. There are still captives to be freed from Satan's prison. There are still those in bondage whom Jesus would release through us. This, too, is part of the gospel commission. This, too, is an important part of the war.

---

1. Acts 10:38
2. Matthew 9:32, 33
3. Mark 9:14-27; Matthew 17:14-18
4. Mark 5:1-20
5. Luke 4:18; see also Isaiah 61:1
6. GC 516
7. Matthew 8:16, 17
8. GC 514
9. Job 1:6-22
10. GC 517
11. DA 341
12. MH 128
13. MB 119
14. 1T 341, 342
15. John 17:18
16. Acts 10:38
17. Matthew 10:1
18. Luke 9:1
19. Mark 16:15-17
20. DA 823
21. EW 227
22. MH 106 (emphasis supplied)
23. TDWG 30
24. EW 191, 192
25. 2SG 277

# Chapter 3
# No King's X

"While men are ignorant of his devices, this vigilant foe [Satan] is upon their track every moment."[1]

This statement from the pen of Mrs. White has important implications. Since Satan is stalking us at all times, he must concern himself with every aspect of human experience. He involves himself in everything we do. This means that in the great controversy there are no "off hours," no "time out."

When I was a boy, children used to yell, "King's X," when they wanted to take time out from a game of tag or hide-and-seek. But there is no "King's X" in this war. Every living person, Christian and non-Christian, is involved in the battle every minute of every day of every year of his life.

## Satan Concerns Himself With Everything Everywhere

The enemy makes it his business to concern himself with every facet of our lives, even with that which may seem to be trivial and inconsequential. He does this because he knows, as God does, that seemingly unimportant things are often more significant than we realize. The so-called "little things" of life often exert an influence upon us and others which is out of proportion to their apparent importance. The "little things" may indicate more accurately than the "larger things" whose side we are really on in this spiritual conflict.

Satan and his demonic forces are everywhere. We cannot escape their presence, although they do not usually make themselves visible to human eyes. They are in our homes. They are walking the streets of our cities and towns. They are in our legislative bodies and in our courts of justice. They attend the religious services in our churches. They are everywhere, doing their mischief, ruining the souls and bodies of men, women, and children.[2] These facts, too, are part of the reality of the war.

Paul revealed the real ramifications of this conflict with this counsel: "Whether therefore ye eat, or drink, or *whatsoever ye do*, do all to the glory of God."[3] Paul is telling us that in every thing we do, even in our eating and drinking, we give glory either to God or to Satan. Everything we think and say and do has a bearing upon the battle. "God expects those who bear the name of Christ to represent Him. . . . *The religion of Christ is to be interwoven with all they do and say.*"[4] In the controversy, there is no "no man's land." C.S. Lewis expressed it in these words: "There is no neutral ground in the universe: every square inch, every split second, is claimed by God and counterclaimed by Satan."[5]

## Satan and the Church

Some people are bothered by the fact that Satan is as successful as he is in his warfare against professing Christians. How can Satan harass, control, and in some cases possess church members? We may not be able to understand the answer to this question completely, but consideration of the following points will give us at least some insights as to the answer.

*Demonic harassment.* In the first place, the Bible plainly teaches that Christians can be harassed or annoyed by Satan. This is one of the most obvious facts revealed in Scripture.

Most of us probably think of Job's experience as the classic example of harassment. While Job was not a Christian in the New Testament meaning of the word, he was a servant of the God of heaven. The Bible describes him as "perfect and upright, and one that feared God, and eschewed [hated or avoided] evil."[6] Yet few people have been harassed as he was. We can understand Job's experience only as we see it in the light of the great controversy that was going on during Job's lifetime, and is still being fought today.

John the Baptist was another "church member" who was subjected to satanic harassment, although it was of a different nature. Jesus said that "there hath not risen a greater than John the Baptist."[7] Yet while he languished in prison "there were hours when the whisperings of demons tortured his spirit, and the shadow of a terrible fear crept over him."[8] Fear and doubt are common forms of demonic harassment today, just as they were in the days of John the Baptist.

The early Christian church was constantly harassed, first by unbelieving Jews, and then by the Roman government. Both of these groups unwittingly allowed Satan to use them for his purpose.

Not only was the church collectively harassed, but individuals within the church experienced harassment. Paul is an example. He writes of having "a thorn in the flesh, the messenger of Satan to buffet me, lest I should be exalted above measure."[9] Paul understood that God was allowing Satan to buffet or harass him (probably through some form of eye disorder) in order to keep him from becoming proud.

James and Ellen White experienced demonic harassment a number of times. Ellen writes how on one occasion Satan harassed her with a "crushing weight" of despair until she could not pray, and she began to doubt if God had really accepted her. She could not so much as lift her eyes to heaven. She suffered intense anguish of mind until her husband interceded on her behalf. Even then, she wrote, "He [Satan] would not yield until my voice was united with his for deliverance."[10]

During one period of Satanic harassment, Mrs. White's head became so swollen that "both eyes were closed, and her face was so disfigured that it no longer looked like that of a human being."[11] Relief came only when Elders White and Loughborough interceded on her behalf.

Satanic harassment of ministers and church leaders is not unknown today. Elder Joel Tompkins, President of the Mid-American Union Conference, related in a sermon an experience in which he was called to intercede in spiritual warfare on behalf of a worker who was being terribly harassed by demons.[12]

Harassment may take many forms, just as it did in Job's case. Physical pain and sickness, financial reverses, and loss of property—all of which Job experienced—are common forms of harassment today. Discouragement and depression are also forms of harassment. One of the most common is fear, which originated with sin and Satan. "God hath not given us the spirit of fear; but of power, and of love, and of a sound mind."[13] We have no reason to fear when we have a true love for God and a faith in Him, because "perfect love casteth out fear."[14]

The obvious purpose of harassment is to discourage the victim, to cause loss of faith and trust in God, and to cause the victim to blame God for the harassment. Satan wants his victim to blame God for the harassment. He wants his victim to do just what Mrs. Job suggested that her husband do: "Curse God, and die."[15]

It is quite evident that committed Christians can be harassed by satanic forces. In fact, the Bible says, "All that will live godly in Christ Jesus shall suffer persecution."[16] If we consider persecution as a form of harassment, we might well ask ourselves why we are not experiencing more harassment than we are. Could it be that the lines of distinction between us and the world are not as clear as they should be? At least it is something to think about.

The antidote for harassment is a strong and abiding faith and trust in God. But maintaining such faith is not always easy when one is suffering physical or emotional pain over a long period of time, which is often the case in severe harassment. Much prayer, reading the word, and claiming God's promises help to maintain strength at such times.

Another essential source of strength and encouragement during these times is the prayers and sympathy of fellow believers. Unfortunately, it is often during periods of severe harassment—when there is sickness or trouble in the family, when one's faith is being tested—that fellow Christians, not always understanding or realizing the true nature of the battle, withdraw their support and loyalty. Without realizing it, they may even become critical of the one who most needs their sympathetic prayers and support just at that time. It is in such cases that we must show that we are indeed a "caring church."

*Demonic control.* Committed Christians may not only be harassed by Satan; they may be temporarily *controlled* by the same enemy. Peter, the most prominent of the twelve disciples, had such an experience near the close of Christ's ministry. The incident is recorded in Matthew 16:21-23. When Jesus attempted to reveal to His disciples "how that he must go unto Jerusalem, and suffer many things of the elders and chief priests and scribes, and be killed, and be raised again the third day," Peter rebuked Him for it.

But it was not really Peter who spoke those words of rebuke. Satan was at that time controlling Peter's mind. Peter was by nature an impulsive man. Satan took advantage of Peter's weakness and caused him presumptuously to contradict Christ's statement. Although he did not realize it, Peter was momentarily under Satan's control, giving voice to Satan's thoughts. But Jesus detected Satan's presence and influence; and in His reply to Peter, He addressed the real spokesman: "Get thee behind me, Satan."[17]

Perhaps God allowed this experience to come to Peter in order that both Peter and we who should live after him might realize how subtle Satan is and how dependent we are upon Christ at all times. Satan takes advantage of our individual weaknesses now just as he did in Peter's time. Satan is no less skillful now than he was then. On the contrary, his skills have been sharpened by two thousand years of additional practice, and to our shame, Satan often uses us as his agents to hurt those who did not intend to injure us—just as he used Peter. Who of us cannot recall saying something which hurt another, which we later regretted, and which we later realized did not come from the right source? Like Peter, we, too, can come under Satan's control unless we are constantly on our guard. This fact is another reality of the war.

### Satan Hates Us

An important factor in Satan's warfare against church members is the special hatred he has toward them and the special effort he puts forth to exercise his control over them.

Satan is still the prince of this world.[18] Therefore he looks upon every human being as his lawful subject. He hates every human being made in the image of God,[19] but he has a special hatred for members of the remnant church. They are followers of Jesus Christ whom he hates with a passion that is beyond our human comprehension. Members of the remnant church also recognize the binding claims of God's holy law, including the Sabbath commandment, which Satan also hates. Members of the remnant church have the advantage of the guidance of the gift of prophecy, and they are preparing for Christ's second coming. All this infuriates the enemy beyond measure. Therefore he makes them the objects of his special attacks.[20] "Never is one received into the family of God without exciting the determined resistance of the enemy."[21]

### Satan's Special Instructions

So great is the enemy's hatred toward the members of the remnant church that he has given his demonic forces special instructions regarding them. Satan told his fallen angels, "The sect of Sabbath keepers we hate; they are continually working against us, and taking from us our subjects, to keep the hated law of God. . . . Present the world before them in the most attractive light. . . . We must keep in our ranks all the means of which we can gain control. . . . As they appoint meetings in different places, we are in danger. . . . Cause disturbances and confusion if possible. Destroy love for one another. . . . *Battle every inch of ground.*"[22]

Satan's forces are carrying out their instructions very well.[23] In too many cases, they are accomplishing their mission. How is the war going in your part of the battlefield? How is the battle progressing in your church? Most important of all, how is the battle going on in your own heart? That is where the issue will be resolved. So far as you are concerned, that is where the war will be won or lost.

### Satan Attacks Church Leaders

Satan attacks not only the church and its members in general, but with a special hatred and zeal he attacks those within the church to whom God has given special talents and abilities and who occupy positions of leadership and influence. The more intelligent, talented, and gifted these people are, the harder will Satan work on them in order that he may persuade them to accomplish *his* work and to advance *his* kingdom.[24] We must keep this fact in mind and not be shocked—although we will, of course, be saddened—when we see some of our brightest lights go out and when leaders join the ranks of the enemy. That this has happened and will continue to happen is another reality of the war. Every war, unfortunately, has its casualties.

**Only "Decided Followers of Christ" Are Safe**

We have not yet touched on one of the most important reasons for Satan's success in making church members his captives. His success is due mainly to the unfortunate fact that many who unite with the church do not have a saving relationship with Jesus Christ. They have united with the church, but not with the Saviour. Not all names registered in the books of the church are registered in the books of heaven.

*Many have been "buried alive."* In 1897 Mrs. White wrote, "The new birth is a rare experience in this age of the world. This is the reason why there are so many perplexities in the church. Many, so many, who assume the name of Christ are unsanctified and unholy. They have been baptized, but they have been buried alive. Self did not die, and therefore they did not rise to newness of life."[25] She also wrote, "The hope of salvation is accepted without a radical change of heart or reformation of life. Thus superficial conversions abound, and multitudes are joined to the church who have never been united to Christ."[26] Is there any good reason to believe these words are less true today than when they were written?

*No one can be neutral in this war.* He who does not yield himself or herself wholly to Jesus Christ is actually under the control of another power—listening to another voice whose suggestions are of an entirely different character. That other power is Satan's, and that other voice is the enemy's, no matter how much we may believe to the contrary. "Satan takes control of every mind that is not decidedly under the control of the Spirit of God."[27]

We must arouse ourselves from the lethargy into which we have fallen and which will destroy us unless we resist it. Satan has a powerful, controlling influence upon many of our minds. All of us—ministers and laypersons alike—are in danger of finding ourselves on the side of the enemy. "There is no such thing now as a neutral position. We are all decidedly for the right or decidedly with the wrong."[28] Jesus told us the same thing: "He that is not with me is against me; and he that gathereth not with me scattereth abroad."[29]

We need not enlist in Satan's army to march under his banner. Failure to serve Jesus completely is to serve Satan. There is no neutral ground. We cannot serve two masters. By virtue of living on the battlefield, we are serving one or the other.

*Nominal church members are not safe.* Not lukewarm Laodiceans or nominal church members, but only those who are decided followers of Christ are safe from Satan's control; for "all who are not decided followers of Christ are servants of Satan."[30] Satan has control of all whom God does not especially guard."[31]

The points covered in this chapter have often been sobering, but nevertheless essential for Seventh-day Adventists to know and understand if victory is to be won. To summarize:

1. The controversy in which we are all involved touches every facet of human experience, even the mundane and seemingly unimportant aspects of life.

2. Satan battles every inch of ground. The absence of battles in the life of a Christian can be a danger signal; for without battles, there can be no victories.

3. Satan has a special hatred for members of the remnant church. Seventh-day Adventists are his special targets in this war.

4. Many members of the remnant church, unfortunately, do not have a saving relationship with Jesus Christ which would protect them from Satan's snares. Therefore they become an easy prey for the enemy.

Given these facts, it is not difficult to understand why

Christians can be harassed, controlled, and even possessed by demonic forces. These facts help me—and I trust that they will help you—understand why Donna (whose experience I related in chapter 1) and many others in similar situations have needed intercessory prayer or spiritual warfare to deliver them from the power of the enemy.

During the past ten years it has been my privilege to pray with and for hundreds of such people, most of whom are members of the church. Among them have been pastors, local elders, musicians, nurses and other professional people, as well as lay persons from various other walks of life. Satan is no respector of persons.

But another important reality of the war is the fact that Jesus is every bit as able to set the captives free today in fulfillment of the gospel commission as He was when He ministered to the needs of the people two thousand years ago. It is this fact that makes victory as much a reality as the war. The war *is* real, *but so is the victory!*

---

1. GC 508
2. GC 508
3. 1 Corinthians 10:31 (emphasis supplied)
4. CT 322 (emphasis supplied)
5. C. S. Lewis, *Christian Relations* (Grand Rapids, Mich.:William B. Erdmans, 1967), p. 33.
6. Job 1:1
7. Matthew 11:11
8. DA 216
9. 2 Corinthians 12:7
10. LS 136
11. John Loughborough, Great Second Advent Movement (Washington, D.C.: Review and Herald Publishing Association, 1905).
12. Sermon preached by Elder Joel Thompkins at Lincoln, Nebraska, November 15, 1986.13. 2 Timothy 1:714. 2 John 4:1815. Job 2:916. 2 Timothy 3:12
17. DA 416; 2 SM 353; 5 BC 1095
18. John 12:31; 14:30; 16:11
19. FE 299
20. EW 192

21. PK 585
22. EW 266, 267 (emphasis supplied)
23. EW 267
24. SDG 336
25. MS 48, 1897
26. GC 468
27. TM 79
28. 3T 328
29. Matthew 12:30
30. GC 508
31. GC 589

# Chapter 4
# Demons You Have Met

It is not always easy to think of demons as being real. Even when the Bible and Mrs. White speak of specific demons, it is easy to feel that the writers are merely employing figures of speech to represent the "carnal nature" with which we were all born. But demons are just as real as we are. They are fallen angels who once lived in heaven and who still have superhuman power and who can resort to supernatural devices. Imitating the human voice or using their victim's vocal chords is one of their many devices.

**Demons Are Real**

Satan, too, is real. Although he has been expelled from heaven, he is still an angel. He has lost his holiness but not his supernatural powers. He still retains his intelligence, but he prostitutes it for the wrong purpose.

The Bible, if we read it carefully, gives us much information about Satan and his angelic forces and their work. The writings of Mrs. White give us additional information in plain terms that we can understand. She tells us, for example, that "Satan assigns to each of his angels a part to act. He enjoins upon them all to be sly, artful, cunning."[1]

We must remember that when she writes of a specific demon—the demon of strife, for example—she is not limiting the name to one specific demon; she is referring to all demons— and there may be millions—who have been assigned the work of causing strife in  world, in the church, and in our homes.

In this chapter I want us to examine some of the demons about whom she writes. Their work is very evident all around us. In my ministry to those who have been oppressed by the enemy, I have heard every one of these—and many others—identify themselves by name. They usually identify themselves by saying, "My name is _____." Or many times they identify themselves by their assignment or work. "My assignment (or work) is _____." With very few exceptions the name indicates the work. When a demonic voice says, "My name is Suicide," it is not necessary to guess what his work or assignment is.

**Demons Named by Mrs. E. G. White**

Let us notice now some of the demons mentioned specifically in the writings of Mrs. White. She tells us, for example, that Jesus knew when He permitted Judas to associate with Him as one of the twelve that Judas was already possessed by a demon of *selfishness*[2] and that he had already surrendered his soul to a demon of *greed*.[3] But in spite of this knowledge, "the Saviour did not repulse Judas. He gave him a place among the twelve. He trusted him to do the work of an evangelist. He endowed him with power to heal the sick and to cast out devils."[4]

Had Judas really opened his heart to Christ in humility and submission, the demons of greed and selfishness would have been cast out. And then Judas, like the other disciples, might have become a citizen in the kingdom of God.[5] But in spite of three years of association with Jesus, Judas never fully surrendered to Him.

There are some important lessons to be learned from Judas's experience. Perhaps the most obvious lesson—but a very important one—is that merely being associated with other Christians and even with Jesus Himself—just knowing about Him but not being surrendered to Him—has no saving power. But isn't that really the experience of many church members? Being a nominal church member is no assurance of a saving relationship with Jesus. Being a nominal church member is detrimental in that it provides a false sense of security. Satan is pleased when we are satisfied with that situation.

From the experience of Judas we also learn that Jesus does not deliver us from Satan's power against our wills. Freedom from Satan's dominance is an important step toward salvation, but Jesus will not help us to take that step against our wills. He will not deny our right to be lost if that is what we choose. That is why the will, which we shall discuss in chapter 6, is so essential in the battle.

A third lesson to be learned from the tragic experience of Judas is that the presence of one cherished sin in the life always opens up the way for other sins. One demon tolerated will invariably make way for others. The demon of greed, harbored in Judas's heart, made way for the demon of suicide; and Judas, instead of repenting of his sin of betrayal, took his own life. Judas became a tragic casualty of the war.

And that brings us to a fourth lesson to be learned from the experience of Judas: In a way that we should never forget, it reminds us of the fact that we are still in the battle. The experience of Judas reminds us that in a war there are gains and there are losses; there are victories and defeats. Even the Saviour experienced the loss of one of His disciples on the battlefield. We are still living on that battlefield, and the war is every bit as real today as it was then.

There is another lesson of a practical nature which we should learn from Jesus' relationship to Judas. Although Jesus knew that Judas was possessed by a demon and needed help, He never approached Judas about that fact. Jesus waited for Judas to come to Him for help, which unfortunately Judas never did. Jesus never forced His ministry upon an unreceptive mind or body.

So in my ministry, I have never approached anyone with the suggestion that he or she "might have a demonic problem." All of those with whom I have engaged in spiritual warfare have asked for help. I believe this is the way it should be. This is in harmony with the example Jesus left for us.

Mrs. White also writes of the demon of *strife,* saying that "if the law of God is obeyed, the demon of strife will be kept out of the family."[6] This demon is successfully working in too many Christian homes today. Every experienced pastor has been called upon to settle domestic problems and to arbitrate arguments that have resulted from the work of this demon. However, not all pastors recognize the relationship between these problems and the great controversy. Therefore, in many cases an attempt is made to solve the problems purely on a human or psychological level. Since Satan is not recognized as the source of the problem, God is too often not recognized as the solution.

And there is a demon of *unkindness*. "Some who profess to be servants of Christ have so long cherished the demon of unkindness that they seem to love the unhallowed element and to take pleasure in speaking words that displease and irritate. These men must be converted before Christ will acknowledge them as His children."[7] It seems obvious that the demons of strife and unkindness often combine their efforts in the same home.

Just as surely as there are demons of strife and unkindness, so there are demons of *divorce*, although I have not found that name in Mrs. White's writings. But I have heard their devilish voices many times during spiritual battles. And demons who operate under the name of Homebreaker are not uncommon. Most of us are aware of their increased activity in Christian homes during recent years. I remember one young woman from whom voices of Divorce and Homebreaker spoke during our prayer session. You can begin to realize how active and successful they had been when I tell you that she had been married and divorced three times. She was still in her midthirties.

## Demons Are Concerned With Our Appetites

One of the most commonly encountered demons is *intemperance*. He "is of giant strength, and is not easily conquered."[8] Those who have had to battle this enemy know how strong he is. Victory over him does not come without a struggle. Incidentally, the statement that this demon "is of giant strength" indicates that not all demons are equally strong, a fact that is evidenced by their different responses during spiritual battle. Although they never leave voluntarily, some demons put up more of a fight than others.

Closely related in work with the demon of intemperance which Mrs. White writes about is the demon of *appetite*, whose voice I have heard identifying himself many times. They may be one and the same demon; at least their goals are similar.

It was not an accident nor a coincidence that the first temptation presented to the human family in the Garden of Eden and the first temptation of Christ in the wilderness was on the point of appetite. As we come closer to the end of time, Satan's temptations to indulge the appetite will be more powerful and more difficult to overcome. Satan knows that *"if he can control the appetite, he can control the whole man."*[9] For that reason he assigns many of his helpers to tempt us in this sensitive area. And in too many cases they are successful in carrying out their assignment in spite of the abundance of light God has given us on that subject.

There are other demons who work in areas related to appetite. Demon *alcohol* is one of them. "Indulgence in intoxicating liquor places a man [or woman] wholly under the control of the demon who devised this stimulant in order to deface and destroy the moral image of God."[10] And the demon who devised alcohol was none other than Satan himself. It was he who suggested converting into poisons, grapes and wheat and other good things given by God to be used as food. In this way he would ruin man's physical, mental, and moral powers and so overcome man's senses that Satan and his demonic forces could have full control.[11] "In dealing with the victims of intemperance [users of alcohol] we must remember that we are not dealing with sane men [or women], but with those who for the time being are under the power of a demon."[12]

Another enemy who works in cooperation with the demon of appetite (and who sometimes operates under that name) is the demon of *nicotine*. I have heard his voice shouting his protests against having to leave his victim many times during spiritual battle. Writing about him, Mrs. White says, "Men professing godliness offer their bodies upon Satan's altar, and burn the incense of tobacco to his satanic majesty. . . . The offering must be presented to some deity. As God is pure and holy, and will accept nothing defiling in its character, He refuses this expensive, filthy, and unholy sacrifice; therefore we conclude that Satan is the one who claims the honor."[13] At times this demon identifies himself as Nicotine, Tobacco, Habit, or Craving. But his work is always the same, to create a desire to use tobacco.

I remember very well an experience that took place while I was engaged in spiritual battle with Paula, a young Adventist woman who, of course, did not smoke. But before we entered into the prayer session, she complained of an almost overwhelming desire to buy some cigarettes. Later, as we were praying, a voice speaking through her said, "Get me a cigarette." I continued to pray, "Lord, you know that Paula does not smoke. Rebuke this demon and cast him out." The voice continued to speak for a few seconds, saying, "I know Paula does not smoke. She knows that it is wrong, but I am trying to convince her that it is all right." Then the demonic voice was silent. I praise God for His power over the enemy. Writing about the smoking habit, Mrs. White says, "It has Satan for its advocate."[14]

### Demon of Masturbation

One of the most powerful demons—and one of the most commonly encountered in my experience—is the demon of *masturbation*. He operates in men and women as well as in boys and girls. What we call masturbation or autostimulation today was called "secret sin" or "master passion" in Mrs. White's day. This practice was the beginning of the downfall of the demoniac of Capernaum.[5] Masturbation, also called "self abuse," was common among the children and young people of some churches in Mrs. White's time. "Right here in this church," she wrote, "corruption is teeming on every hand." She went on to say that "the minds of some of these children are so weakened that they have but one half or one third of the brilliancy of intellect that they might have had had they been virtuous and pure. They have thrown it away in self-abuse."[16]

The problem of masturbation and its results is one area in which medical science and psychology have not yet "caught up" with divine revelation. Some psychologists and secular writers advocate the practice of masturbation as a means of releasing inner tensions. I am afraid that some Christian psychologists, even among our own people, have fallen into this same trap.

In contrast to this concept, let us look briefly at God's counsel. "Some who make a high profession do not understand the sin of self-abuse and its sure results. Long-established habit has blinded their understanding. They do not realize the exceeding sinfulness of this degrading sin. . . . Many professed Christians are so benumbed by the same practice that their moral sensibilities cannot be aroused to understand that it is sin, and that if continued its sure results will be utter shipwreck of body and mind."[17]

I have intentionally dealt with this subject at some length because my experience in spiritual warfare indicates that the demon of masturbation is every bit as active today as when Mrs. White wrote her counsel.

As powerful and active as this demon is, he gives way in the presence of loyal angels and the Holy Spirit when the door of faith opens the heart to the Saviour. Even the demons who possessed the demoniac of Capernaum "came out of him."[18]

But parents need to be alert to this danger and do everything possible to safeguard their children from this habit. Then they can claim the promise, "Thus saith the Lord, Even the captives of the mighty shall be taken away, and the prey of the terrible shall be delivered: for I will contend with him that contendeth with thee, and I will save thy children."[19]

### Jealousy

As we conclude this chapter, let us consider one other demon named in the writings of Mrs. White. You will remember that the record says King Saul became very upset when at the end of a certain battle the women of Israel sang, "Saul hath slain his thousands, and David his ten thousands."[20] Saul became angry because David was exalted above him, and "the demon of jealousy entered the heart of the king."[21] Pride and jealousy were among Satan's original sins in heaven, and we can be sure that he is doing his best to cause human beings to commit the same sins today. And too often he is successful, even among church members and church officers. How he must gloat over that victory!

**Legions of Demons**

We have considered in this chapter some of the demons mentioned in the writings of Mrs. White. All these and many others I have heard during spiritual battles. "Whole legions of devils are watching their opportunities to get hold of human minds."[22] She writes of Satan's "evil train of impatience, love of self, pride, avarice, overreaching, and his whole catalogue of evil spirits."[23]

Commanding this demonic army in military style is Satan, whom Mrs. White refers to as "the demon of heresy," saying that he "has mapped out the world, and has resolved to possess it as his kingdom. Those who are in his army are numerous. . . . They possess a zeal, tact, and ability that is marvelous, and [they] press their way into every new opening where the standard of truth is uplifted."[24]

Notice her use of personal pronouns: "*his* kingdom," "*his* army," "*they* possess," and "*their* way." Her use of these words shows she was referring to actual beings; she was not speaking of demons as symbols of evil or as any other figure of speech. The war is real—and so is the enemy.

1. EW 90
2. 5BC 1102
3. ED 92
4. DA 717
5. DA 294
6. AH 106
7. SL 13
8. T 176
9. T 276 (emphasis supplied)
10. T 32

11. T 12; RH, April 16, 1901
12. MH 172
13. T 63; CH 83; SL 31
14. T 58
15. MH 91-93; DA 255, 256
16. 2T 361
17. CG 441
18. Mark 1:26
19. Isaiah 49:25
20. 1 Samuel 18:7
21. PP 650
22. SDG 196
23. 4T 45
24. UL 275

# Chapter Five
# How to Tempt Satan

Have you ever tempted Satan? Of course we usually think of Satan as tempting us, but at times—and probably more often than we realize—we actually tempt Satan. We invite the enemy to tempt us—we tempt him—whenever we give him the advantage in any way. And Satan, who is always looking for weak spots in our defense, appreciates any help we're willing to give.

There are few ways in which we give Satan more advantage than we do by remaining ignorant of his plans, methods, and devices when God has given us so much light on that matter. "He [Satan] could not gain advantage if his method of attack were understood."[1]

I hope your reading of these pages will alert you to some of the enemy's methods of attack and consequently lessen the advantage he has had in your life thus far. With God's help, you can now begin to tempt Satan less than you have in the past.

In this chapter we are going to consider some specific ways in which we, even as Seventh-day Adventist Christians, tempt Satan and thereby make his work easier. Satan does not deserve any advantage, but we give it to him when we fail to heed the warnings and to use the information God has given.

*Compromise.* As much as in any other way, I suspect that we tempt Satan by "walking carelessly." Mrs. White says that many of us "walk so carelessly" that we become "an easy prey."[2] In other words, *we compromise.* I have heard more

49

than one demonic voice say during spiritual battle, "I can't get into people unless they compromise." It's so easy to compromise—and so dangerous! And since Satan concerns himself with every area of human experience, he does not really care in what area we compromise. Our compromise in any area serves his purpose well. *Every victory the enemy gains involves some degree of compromise.*

*Failure to guard our senses.* A *second* way in which we tempt Satan is by failing to guard our senses. "Those who would not fall a prey to Satan's devices must guard well the avenues of the soul; they must avoid reading, seeing, or hearing that which will suggest impure thoughts."[3]

There are few areas in which we are tempted to compromise more than in what we watch on television. We must remember that the real issue in this war is control of the human mind. I well remember an experience I had a few years ago when an Adventist couple brought their daughter for spiritual battle because she was living in a world of fantasy, largely as a result of watching television. Said one of the demonic voices, *"My name is Television. You know, we demons control the television industry. In fact, we control the whole entertainment industry."*

Remember that the controversy enters into every phase of human experience. How can anyone be so naive as to think, even for a minute, that Satan would not attempt to control any industry that has as much impact on human thought and behavior as television has on society today? Wouldn't it be foolish of him not to control it if he could?

When we compromise the standards God has given us in Philippians 4:8, we tempt Satan to tempt us.

We also tempt Satan when we allow our thoughts and imaginations to go uncontrolled. "The mind should not be left to wander at random upon every subject that the adversary of souls may suggest."[4]

God gave us our imaginations, and there are legitimate uses for them. In fact, God encourages us to use them, but in the right way and for the proper purpose. "Let your imagination take hold upon things unseen. Let your thoughts be directed to the evidences of the great love of God for you."[5] "It would be well for us to spend a thoughtful hour each day in contemplation of the life of Christ. We should take it point by point, and let the imagination grasp each scene, especially the closing ones."[6]

Jesus cautioned that conditions in the world just before He returns will be very much as they were just before the flood, when "every imagination of the thoughts . . . was only evil continually."[7]

*Indolence.* We also tempt Satan when we waste or misuse our time. Actually, of course, time is not ours but God's. Time is the one talent He gives to all of us in equal amounts as long as He gives us life. "Of no talent He [God] has given will He require a more strict account than of our time."[8] In our high-pressure society we sometimes feel that we do not have enough time. But "if every moment were valued and rightly employed, we should have time for everything that we need to do for ourselves or for the world."[9] It is necessary today to spend some time in recreation, but God makes a distinction between recreation and amusement, a distinction we often fail to make. True recreation, preferably done in the open air, re-creates us mentally, spiritually, and physically. On the other hand, "amusements are doing more to counteract the working of the Holy Spirit than anything else, and the Lord is grieved."[10]

Yes, "it is wrong to waste our time."[11] "The indolent man tempts the devil to tempt him."[12] This is another area in which we must be on guard, lest we give Satan another advantage.

*Walking on Satan's ground and playing with his toys.* We tempt Satan when we walk on his ground and play with his toys. "If we venture on Satan's ground we have no assurance of protection from his power. So far as in us lies, we should close every avenue by which the tempter may find access to us."[13]

Satan has a number of booby traps, every one of which is deadly, no matter how innocent and attractive it may appear. A partial list of Satan's toys would include the following. You may think of others.

the Ouija board          rock music
astrology                heavy metal music
numerology               tarot cards
magic writing            playing cards
hypnotism                video games
drugs                    novels
alcohol                  pornography

You may question some of the items in this list, playing cards, for example. I see them in some Adventist homes. But card playing is not an activity we can safely take part in; for where there is card playing, there Satan is.[14] Harboring the enemy in the home in time of war is treason, and we are in a very real war. Why should we betray our Saviour by inviting the enemy into our homes? Card playing, along with the gambling that is associated with it, is like alcohol in that it is an invention of the devil.[15] The purpose of both—card playing and alcohol—is to destroy us spiritually. Some have told me that they do not use the cards that are in their homes. Then the question is even more valid, why tempt Satan by taking his toys into our homes? How can a Christian sincerely ask for God's protection under those conditions?

The games, the books, and the magazines we have in our homes do matter, and some of our people have had to learn this the hard way. In my ministering to those who were suffering demonic oppression, I have heard demonic voices say, "I don't have to leave. She has invited me into her home. Look in the bookcase." More than one family has had to do some "house cleaning" before they were delivered from Satan's influence.

Some of us not only play with Satan's toys; we walk on his ground. We walk on Satan's ground when we bargain with him, pray to him, or become involved in any form of spiritualism or witchcraft. And if you think that Adventist young people—at least young people coming from Adventist-oriented homes—are not venturing on Satan's ground in these ways, you are very naive.

"Some, I was shown, gratify their curiosity and tamper with the devil. . . . They are venturing on the devil's ground and are tempting him to control them. This powerful destroyer considers them his lawful prey. . . . When they wish to control themselves they cannot. They yielded their minds to Satan, and he will not release his claims, but holds them captive."[16]

Several years ago I received a phone call for help from a young Adventist man who had become deeply involved in numerology, but who now wanted out. Numerology is the belief that one's life is controlled by numbers or number combinations in much the same way that some people believe their lives are controlled by the position of heavenly bodies. This man was so controlled by numerology that he had given up a good job "because the number told me to."

When he called, he said he wanted help; but he was so caught in Satan's web that he was not receptive to help. He lived in fear. He was afraid of "what the numbers told him," and he was afraid of what would happen if he ignored the numbers.

Satan controlled his entire life. If I read a Bible promise to him over the phone, for example, his response invariably was, "What page is it on? What is the number?" Even when I pointed out that the text might be on a different page in another Bible, it made no difference. I am sorry to have to tell you that a few weeks later he hanged himself in his garage. Satan truly holds captive those who walk on his ground and play with his toys.

*Seeking counsel from non-Christians.* We run the risk of tempting Satan and placing ourselves and our children under his influence, when we seek professional help from non-Christians. Charlene's experience is a good illustration of this. She came for help because "another power" seemed to be in control of her life, and that power was "not good." She was an Adventist, but she had grown up in a divided home with a mother who had taken her to a Christian Science practitioner rather than to a medical doctor. When she shared this information during our pre-prayer session, I did not attach too much importance to it.

But while we were praying in spiritual battle a little later, five different voices said, in effect, "I have been in her since she was a child. I got in her when her mother took her to a Christian Science practitioner."

To God's glory I can say that Charlene was delivered from the satanic control under which she had been living, but it required several sessions of spiritual battle.

A few weeks later, I ran across the following paragraph which helped me to understand the significance of what we had experienced:

"There are many who shrink with horror from the thought of consulting spirit mediums, but who are attracted by more pleasing forms of spiritism. Others are led astray by the teachings of Christian Science, and by the mysticism of Theosophy and other Oriental religions. . . . And there are not a few, even in this Christian age, who go to these healers, instead of trusting in the power of the living God and the skill of well-qualified physicians. The mother . . . is told of the wonderful cures performed by some clairvoyant or magnetic healer, and she trusts her dear one to his charge, *placing it as verily in the hand of Satan as if he were standing by her side. In many instances the future of the child is controlled by a satanic power which it seems impossible to break.*"[17]

Charlene's experience is not as uncommon as you may think. I have prayed in spiritual battle for others who have experienced problems similar to Charlene's because they discovered too late that they had consulted with those who were involved in astrology, hypnotism and witchcraft. It is always dangerous to walk on Satan's ground.

**Demons in the Home**

Every war has certain areas where the fighting is more severe than elsewhere. Consequently, those areas suffer the greatest number of casualties. Perhaps there is no place in the great controversy where the battle is more severe, where Satan tempts us more, or where we tempt him more, than in our homes. Home is where we relax. Home is where we are most likely to be our natural selves. And that is the problem! Home is where the "natural self," the carnal man, is likely to show himself. Home is where we show what we really are. "It is from your conduct at your home that we shall be able to judge in a large measure whether or not you are a real Christian."[18]

We tempt Satan and open the door to him when we speak cross words in the home. "It is natural for human beings to speak sharp words. Those who yield to this inclination open the door for Satan to enter their hearts."[19] The good angels flee from homes where there are unpleasant words, fretfulness, and strife.[20] "All jangling and unpleasant, impatient, fretful words are an offering presented to his satanic majesty."[21] It would be well for each of us to pray as David did, "Set a watch, O Lord, before my mouth; keep the door of my lips."[22]

We also tempt Satan when we permit our children to grow up in *permissive homes.* A permissive home is one in which the father and mother have abandoned their God-given parental privileges and responsibilities, and permit the children to set the standards and make the rules. This is happening in too many Christian homes today, and compromise always results. We have all seen little children kick and scream and throw themselves on the floor in a temper tantrum. In commenting on this behavior, Mrs. White makes this observation: "This is the time *to rebuke the evil spirit.* The enemy will try to control the minds of our children, but why shall we allow him to mold them according to his will?"[23]

We are in a real war; and as in any war, time is of the essence. Therefore Satan begins to work upon children's minds as soon as they are born, and in some cases, even before they are born.

Before I entered the preaching ministry, I spent a number of years in the teaching ministry in our denominational school system. We teachers used to talk about children whom we thought were "undisciplined." I have since learned that there is no undisciplined child. Every child is disciplined; it is simply a matter of who does the disciplining. In writing about these children from poorly governed, permissive homes, Mrs. White says, "The enemy will work right through those children, unless they are disciplined. Someone disciplines them. *If the mother or the father does not do it, the devil does.* That is how it is. He has the control.[24]

We tempt Satan, too, when we fail to uphold God's standards in our homes by precept and by example. We have seen that Satan will discipline children in *his* school if the parents neglect to discipline them in *their* homes. In the same way, Satan will take over other duties which the parents neglect. "Unless parents plant the seeds of truth in the hearts of their children, the enemy will sow tares."[25]

It behooves us to do all we can in cooperation with God to make our homes as free as possible from the enemy's snares—a miniature city of refuge for our children as well as for ourselves.

We are all involved in a life-and-death struggle. But God has made it possible for each one of us to experience victory, which is just as real as the battle. We have not been left to fight the battle alone. Jesus Christ is still Lord and Saviour. The devils are still subject to us through His name. When we do our part in this battle, when we surrender to Jesus Christ and submit ourselves entirely to Him, He will do for us what we cannot do for ourselves. But there is a work which we must do.

"Those who have tempted the devil to tempt them will have to make desperate efforts to free themselves from his power. But *when they begin to work for themselves,* then angels of God whom they have grieved will come to their rescue."[26]

Would you like to begin right now to "work for yourself" so that angels of God will come to your rescue? You can begin by telling Jesus that you want to surrender completely to Him. If you cannot do anything else, you can ask Jesus to make you willing to be made willing.

I would like to encourage you to take one more step in the right direction. If you have a marriage partner, talk with your spouse about your new determinations and desires. Invite him or her to join you in presenting a united front to the enemy. Unite your wills and your hearts in establishing the family altar in your home. Gather your family around you for morning and evening worship if you are not already doing that. This will go a long way toward making you and your family impregnable to Satan's attacks.

Determine that with God's grace you are not going to allow even one crack to appear in the wall of defense around your home. *If there is even one crack, Satan will get in.* That, unfortunately, is another reality of the war.

---

1. 1T 308
2. UL 34
3. PP 460
4. PP 460
5. MH 488
6. DA 83
7. Genesis 6:5
8. COL 342
9. MYP 322; MH 208
10. MYP 371
11. MYP 322
12. OHC 222
13. MB 118
14. 4T 652; AH 517, 518; CH 197
15. CS 134
16. 1T 299
17. PK 210, 211; Ev. 606; RH, Jan. 15, 1914 (emphasis supplied)
18. RH, July 2, 1889
19. AH 441
20. 1T 307
21. 1T 310
22. Psalm 141:3
23. *Home Education*, 1893 (a pamphlet) (emphasis is supplied)
24. 3 SM 218 (emphasis supplied)
25. 1MCP 15
26. 1T 301 (emphasis supplied)

# Chapter Six
# Our Kingly Power

One human factor outweighs all others in determining the outcome of the great controversy on the personal level. And the personal level, we must remember, is the only level on which victory can be gained. This all-important element is the human will.

When God created Adam and Eve, He made them after His likeness.[1] "Human beings were a new and distinct order. They were made 'in the image of God' "![2]

One of Adam's and Eve's Godlike qualities was the capacity to develop characters patterned after the character of God Himself. This capacity distinguishes us human beings from all other forms of animal life. It is "the will" that makes character formation possible.

### The Will Is the Governing Power

Sometimes we think of the will as the power of choice. But the will involves much more than choice. The will is the governing power which God gives to every normal human being to control all the other faculties and powers which God has given to us. In this war in which we are all engaged, "everything depends upon the right action of the will."[3]

The will is not to lie dormant. Proper use of the will requires that it be constantly exercised.

Man's will was given to him when he was created. But when man sinned, his will came under Satan's control. And ever since the fall, Satan has been using our wills contrary to

our best interest in order to carry out *his* will and to accomplish *his* purpose. But the sacrifice Jesus made on the
cross in order to redeem us from Satan's control gives God a
legal right to take control of our wills again if we will yield
them to Him for that purpose. Then He can work in us to will
and to do of *His* good pleasure.[4]

There are only two things we can do with our wills:

1. Refuse to yield our wills to Jesus, which means that
Satan will continue to exercise the control he gained at the
fall.

2. Surrender our wills to Jesus Christ.

There really is no third choice. It is not necessary for us to
choose intentionally to serve the enemy in order to come
under his control; "we have only to neglect to ally ourselves
with the kingdom of light."[5] *We do not have to enlist in Satan's
army in order to march under his banner.* We were born under
his banner, and we shall continue to march under his banner,
and we shall suffer destruction with him unless we deliberately *will* to march under the banner of Jesus Christ. And that
choice must be made not once, but every day; and sometimes
it must be made every hour or every minute when we are
under the enemy's attack.

Some of the most encouraging and remarkable statements
in the writings of Mrs. White have to do with our wills—the
kingly power God has given to us. The following two short
paragraphs are examples:

"As the will of man co-operates with the will of God, it [the
will of man] becomes *omnipotent.*"[6]

"When the soul surrenders itself to Christ, a new power
takes possession of the new heart. A change is wrought which
man can never accomplish for himself. It is a supernatural
work, *bringing a supernatural element into human nature.* . . .
A soul thus kept in possession by the heavenly agencies is *impregnable to the assaults of Satan.*"[7]

## A Life of Victory Is Possible

Think for a few minutes what God is saying here. He is telling us that when we surrender completely to His will, our

human wills, which are naturally weak and wavering, take on the Godlike characteristic of omnipotence. God knows that we can never defeat Satan in our human strength. But when we yield our wills completely to His, He has a legal right to give us supernatural power to fight supernatural enemies. This "supernatural element" then makes us impregnable to the assaults of Satan so long as we are totally surrendered to Him. Our victory in this controversy depends entirely upon our meshing our human wills with the divine will of God. *There is no other way to escape defeat.* "The only hope for us if we would overcome is to unite our will to God's will and work in cooperation with Him, hour by hour and day by day."[8]

"A pure and noble life, a life of victory over appetite and lust, is possible for everyone who will unite his weak, wavering human will to the omnipotent, unwavering will of God."[9]

It is not by our own determination, not by the gritting of our teeth, that the victory is gained, but by "yielding up" our wills to Jesus Christ. In this war, victory is assured only as we surrender. And we must do the surrendering, for God will not take our wills by force. For Him to do so would mean that we are no longer made in His image, with the capacity to develop characters patterned after His. For God to use force would substantiate Satan's claim that God is a tyrant who ignores our wills and desires.

It is not the work of the good angels to force our wills.[10] And Satan himself does not have the power to do it.[11] God *will not* violate our wills, and Satan *cannot.* Only we can decide what shall be done with the kingly power which God has entrusted to us.

Although Satan cannot force our wills, he has many subtle ways of gaining control of both our wills and our minds without our being aware of it unless we are constantly on guard. He has been experimenting with the properties of the human mind for thousands of years, and he knows how to use this experience to his advantage. He imbues human minds with his thoughts and ideas in such a subtle way that those who are gradually coming under his spell think they are carrying out *their own* ideas and doing *their* will.

The enemy's purpose in all this is to so confuse the minds of men and women and boys and girls that they eventually will hear no voice but his. Satan's sly suggestions first infiltrate, then contaminate, and eventually, if the enemy has his way, they will dominate. In previous chapters we have discussed some of the devices and methods he uses to accomplish his purpose.

**A Basic Principle.**

It is essential that we remember that more than any other factor, our wills determine our victory or defeat in this most important of all wars. There is a basic principle which we must all understand if we expect to gain the victory. That principle is this: *Whenever we knowingly and intentionally go contrary to what we know is God's revealed will for us, we are yielding some of our will to the enemy. Whenever we deliberately do anything which we know is displeasing to God, we turn some of our kingly power over to Satan.* And each time we do this, it becomes easier for us to do it again. When we reject light and do what we know is contrary to God's will for us, "the eyes are blinded and the heart [is] hardened. Often the process is gradual, and almost imperceptible. . . . When one ray of light is disregarded, there is a partial benumbing of the spiritual perception, and the second revealing of light is less clearly discerned" (DA 322, 323). "Every ray of light neglected leaves the sinner in greater darkness than before, till some fearful deception may take possession of his mind, and his case may become hopeless."[12] Millions of people in every walk of life, in the world and in the church are doing this today.

But we have not been left to Satan's mercy. "He [Christ] came to expel the demons that had controlled the will. He came to lift us up from the dust, to reshape the marred character after the pattern of His divine character, and to make it beautiful with His own glory."[13]

Jesus came to make it possible for each of us to have victory over the enemy. This is what Jesus was saying when He read at Nazareth, "The Spirit of the Lord is upon me, because he hath anointed me to preach the gospel to the poor; he hath sent me to heal the brokenhearted, to preach deliverance to the captives, and recovering of sight to the blind, to set at liberty them that are bruised."[14]

When we give our consent for Jesus to take control of our wills, He will so identify His will with our thoughts and aims, so blend our hearts and minds into conformity to His Word, that in obeying His will, we will only be carrying out the impulses of our minds.[15] At one with Christ, we can claim His victory as our victory.

Together, we are more than a match for Satan!

---

1. Genesis 1:26, 27
2. 1 BC 1081; SDG 7; RH, Feb. 11, 1902
3. SC 47
4. MYP 153, 154; 5T 513, 514
5. DA 324
6. COL 333 (emphasis supplied)
7. DA 324 (emphasis supplied)
8. MB 143
9. MH 176
10. MYP 53
11. GC 510
12. 3 SP 159
13. DA 38
14. Luke 4:18
15. UL 187

# Chapter 7
# The Victory Is Real Too!

It is quite evident that there are different levels or degrees of demonic influence in human experience. I think of Satan's work as being under four different levels: (1) temptation (2) harassment (3) control (4) possession. Since I have discussed harassment and control in chapter 3, I shall limit this chapter to temptation, and discuss possession in chapter 9.

## Temptation Is Deadly

In terms of the suffering and trauma it produces, temptation may be considered the least severe level of satanic oppression. *But it is also the most dangerous,* for it is in temptation that demonic control and possession take root and flourish. Temptation always precedes control and possession. A second dangerous aspect of temptation is that it is so much a part of our experience that it is easy to take it for granted—to accept it as part of life's normal experience and to forget that it is demonic. But temptation is every bit as deadly today as it was in the Garden of Eden.

No matter how innocent or sophisticated temptation may appear, it always comes from the enemy. Temptation never comes from God, although He obviously permits it for reasons which we shall discuss later in this chapter. "Let no man say when he is tempted, I am tempted of God: for God cannot be tempted with evil, neither tempteth he any man."[1]

Satan knows better than we do that "the wages of sin is death."[2] So one of his important goals is to entice us into sin and then—by procrastination, carelessness, death, or any means he can use—to prevent our sins from being confessed and covered with the blood of Jesus. In this way he hopes to bring about our eternal destruction.

Satan knows, too, that he can never be saved. He has nothing to lose in this conflict that he has not already lost. Therefore, he resorts to any tactic, device, or plan that will accomplish his purpose, no matter how deceitful or cruel it may be. He is earnest, zealous, and persevering in his work. If he fails to accomplish his purpose one time, he will try again. He will lay other plans and work with a determination that is worthy of a more noble cause in order to ensnare souls. "He never becomes so discouraged as to let souls entirely alone."[3]

This enticing into sin we call temptation, and it comes in an unlimited number of forms. I would like to suggest two definitions of temptation, each from a different point of view.

*From Satan's point of view,* temptation is any means he is permitted to use to entice us into sin in order to accomplish his purpose of bringing about our eventual eternal destruction.

*From God's point of view,* temptation is the circumstance He permits to arise in a sinful world in order to give us an opportunity to prove our loyalty to Him and to develop and strengthen our characters.

God permits us to be tempted, not because He takes pleasure in the resultant distress of Satan's enticements, but because exposure to temptation is necessary for our ultimate victory. God "could not, consistently with His own glory, shield them [His people] from temptation; for the very object of the trial is to prepare them to resist all the allurements of evil."[4] "God permits temptation to come to His people today, that they may realize that He is their helper. If they draw nigh to Him when they are tempted, He strengthens them to meet the temptation. But if they yield to the enemy, neglecting to place themselves close to their Almighty Helper, they are overcome. . . . They do not give evidence that they walk in God's way."[5]

The Bible suggests this same attitude toward temptation in these words:

Wherein ye greatly rejoice, though now for a season, if need be, ye are in heaviness through manifold temptations: that the trial of your faith, being much more precious than of gold that perisheth, though it be tried with fire, might be found unto praise and honour and glory at the appearing of Jesus Christ."[6]

Although temptation may be a real trial and may bring heaviness of heart temporarily, we should rejoice for the opportunity to prove our loyalty to our Saviour.

"When a man [or any person] is filled with the Spirit, the more severely he is tested and tried, the more clearly he proves that he is a representative of Christ."[7] This of course does not mean that we are to invite temptation so that we may have an opportunity to prove our loyalty to God. This would be presumptuous and, as we discussed in chapter five, to tempt Satan to tempt us is a foolish and dangerous thing to do.

### Temptation Is Not Sin

It is important to recognize, however, that it is not a sin to be tempted. Jesus "was in all points tempted like as we are, yet without sin."[8] Temptation and sin are two different and distinct human experiences, but they are so closely related that it is important that we be able to distinguish between the two.

I would suggest that temptation becomes sin when we begin to enjoy the temptation and to toy with it. David's sin with Bathsheba did not begin when he inadvertently saw a woman bathing. His sin began when he lingered to enjoy the view.

### How to Handle Snakes

There is only one way to handle the snakes of temptation properly. That is to follow Paul's example. We must do what he did when the snake fastened itself to his arm when he was helping to build the fire after the shipwreck on the island of Melita.[9] Paul did not take time to rationalize, to justify the snake's presence, or to appoint a committee to study the situation. Paul did the only safe thing to do with any snake; he shook it off immediately.

The Bible gives us the example of another man who had an experience with a different kind of snake. His name was Joseph, and the snake was in the form of the seductive charms of Mrs. Potiphar. The Bible tells us how Joseph reacted to that snake of temptation. He said, "How then can I do this great wickedness, and sin against God?" "He left his garment in her hand, and got him out."[10]

Joseph did not linger to enjoy the view. He shook off the snake just as Paul did. But the most important lesson we can learn from Joseph's experience is this: Joseph's ability to resist that temptation was not an accident. *It was the result of his having made a complete surrender to God.*

Between the time his brothers sold him and the time he arrived in Egypt, Joseph had an opportunity to do some serious soul-searching. He might have rationalized that since God had allowed him to be sold into slavery, there was obviously no point in serving Him any longer. Or he might have felt that since he was now among strangers, he could "eat, drink, and be merry," and no one would know or care. But Joseph did neither of these. Instead, during that long, lonely journey down to Egypt, Joseph *"gave himself fully to the Lord."*[11]

Everyone who makes the same full commitment to the Lord that Joseph made can resist temptation as Joseph did and can live the victorious life that Joseph lived. You and I can have that same victorious experience. "To everyone who surrenders fully to God is given the privilege of living without sin, in obedience to the law of heaven."[12]

That statement is from the pen of Mrs. White, but the idea that it is possible for Christians to live without committing intentional and known sin did not originate in her mind. That concept originated in God's mind, and He tells us that in many places in His Word. "Knowing this, that our old man is crucified with him [Christ], that the body of sin might be destroyed, *that henceforth we should not serve sin. For he that is dead* [fully surrendered] is *freed from sin.*"[13]

Other verses teach the same truth.[14]

## God's High Standard

God's standard for us is very high. "Godliness—godlikeness—is the goal to be reached."[15] The Bible uses another word—*blameless*—in describing the same standard. "The very God of peace sanctify you wholly; and I pray God your whole spirit and soul and body be preserved blameless unto the coming of our Lord."[16]

To be "godlike" and "blameless" is a higher standard than any of us can reach. All the good intentions we may have, all the promises we may make to ourselves or to God, all the determination we can muster, will not help. There is no way we can reach that standard. I know that, and you know that. But God knows that too. And so immediately after asking us to do the impossible—in the very next verse—he quickly adds, "Faithful is he that calleth you [to this impossibly high standard], *who also will do it.*"[17] Think of it for a moment. God sets the standard high in harmony with His own character which cannot change, but He knows that we can never meet that standard. So He assures us immediately that if we will give Him permission by surrendering fully to Him, He will meet the standard for us. That is good news!

But we must make no mistake about it; God does expect us to gain the victory over temptation and sin here and now. He has made it possible for us to do just that. *Jesus lived a perfect life on the battlefield himself and died on the cross, not that we might learn to live comfortably with our sins, but that through Him we might gain the victory over them.*

To deny the possibility of victory over sin in this life is to deny the purpose of the first advent. "In this earth [Christ] performed his mission, and fulfilled his office, and, by obedience to the law of God, he testified to all its immutable character, while at the same time proving that its precepts could be perfectly obeyed through his grace by every son and daughter of Adam."[18]

The war may be real—and it is—but, thank God, so is the victory!

1. James 1:13
2. Romans 6:23
3. SDG 263
4. GC 528
5. 1BC 1094
6. 1 Peter 1:6, 7
7. OHC 150
8. Hebrews 4:15
9. Acts 28:1-5
10. Genesis 39:9, 12
11. PP 213, 214 (emphasis supplied)
12. RH, Sept. 27, 1906
13. Romans 6:6, 7 (emphasis supplied)
14. See for examples: Romans 6:17, 18; 1 John 3:6, 8, 9
15. ED 18
16. 1 Thessalonians 5:23
17. 1 Thessalonians 5:24 (emphasis supplied)
18. ST, March 14, 1895

# Chapter 8
# Saints on Earth

Since God through Jesus Christ has made it possible for His children to gain the victory over sin, why do so many Christians go on sinning, knowingly doing that which they know is against God's will? Why do so many of us experience spiritual defeat day after day? Why don't more Christians live victorious lives?

**Two Reasons for Defeat**

I suggest that there are two basic reasons. First of all, we do not fully appreciate the sinfulness of sin. We do not realize how utterly detestable sin is; we do not comprehend how contrary sin is to God's character and how terribly offensive it is to Him. We have lived with sin and its results so long and toyed with it so much that for us it has lost much of its horror and repugnance. "We shall not renounce sin unless we see its sinfulness."[1]

The absolute horror of sin can be seen only when we look at the cross. It would be well for us each day to pray that God would give us a genuine abhorrence of sin and a hatred for it because of what it did to the Son of God and because of what it does to us. When we recognize the true nature of sin, we shall no longer crucify to ourselves "the Son of God afresh, and put him to an open shame"[2] by deliberately doing anything we know is displeasing to Him.

But there is a second reason why many Christians are not gaining the victory over temptation and sin. Many are not convinced that victory over sin is possible in this life. In fact, many are convinced that such victory is *impossible*. And that is exactly what Satan wants us to think.

"If those who hide and excuse their faults could see how Satan exults over them, how he taunts Christ and holy angels with their course, they would make haste to confess their sins and to put them away. Through defects in the character, Satan works to gain control of the whole mind, and he knows that if these defects are cherished, he will succeed. Therefore he is constantly seeking to deceive the followers of Christ with his *fatal sophistry* that it is impossible for them to overcome."[3] A "fatal sophistry" is a lie which, if believed, will result in death. And what is this fatal lie which Satan wants us to believe? "That it is impossible for them [the followers of Christ] to overcome." That we cannot, through the power of an indwelling Saviour, overcome temptation and sin in this life is a lie which, if we believe it, will result in our eternal death. And Satan, because he is our deadly enemy in this war, is doing his best to cause every one of us to believe it.

The problem is that many of us try to overcome in our own strength, and this we cannot do. "Without Christ we cannot subdue a single sin or overcome the smallest temptation."[4] Jesus told us the same thing when He said, "Without me ye can do nothing."[5]

### God Does the Impossible

But what we cannot do, God does for us if we surrender to Him and in faith ask Him to do it. That is what justification is all about. "What is justification by faith? It is the work of God in laying the glory of man in the dust, and doing for man that which it is not in his power to do for himself."[6] God, then, does for us everything essential to our salvation which we cannot do for ourselves. And since we can do nothing, He really does it all. The only thing we can do is to give Him permission to do His work by surrendering fully to Him, and then to cooperate with Him in the refining process.

The fact that we must overcome temptation and sin in this

life here and now is one of the plainest teachings in the writings of Mrs. White, as well as of the Bible. One or two short quotations will make the point, although many might be cited.[7]

God "has made provision that the Holy Spirit shall be imparted to every repentant soul, *to keep him from sinning.*"[8]

"He who has not sufficient faith in Christ to believe *that he can keep from sinning,* has not the faith that will give him an entrance into the kingdom of God."[9]

How could the idea be expressed any more plainly in the English language?

Most of us expect that the time will come when we will be able to live without deliberately sinning. We look forward to the time when we will be able to resist every temptation. But that is the problem—we are always looking *forward* to it. That time is always in the future. And that is exactly what Satan wants. It suits his purpose well when we keep putting off the time of victory to some future date.

It is easy for us to believe that somehow we will be changed when Jesus comes to rescue us from the battlefield. But a careful reading of 1 Corinthians 15:53; Philippians 3:21 and related texts plainly shows that the changes which will take place at Christ's second coming will involve only our physical bodies. There will be no changes in our dispositions or our characters at that time. "The transformation of character must take place before His coming."[10]

The dispositions and characters of those who are saved will be the same on the day of Christ's appearing as they were the day before He appears.

"The change from earth to heaven will not change men's characters; the happiness of the redeemed in heaven results from the characters formed in this life, after the image of Christ. The saints in heaven will first have been saints on earth."[11]

## Christian Perfection

Jesus admonished, "Be ye therefore perfect."[12] But He obviously was not talking about absolute perfection, as some suppose; for absolute perfection is not attainable to any created being, but only to God. Had the angels been perfect in the absolute sense, there would have been no rebellion in heaven.

Some Christians, not understanding this, have despaired of ever reaching the goal of perfection and have given up. Others have assumed that whatever degree of perfection God requires will be realized only after Jesus comes and "changes us." Still others have rationalized that all of our need for perfection is met in Christ and that when they accept Him, they need not be concerned any further about perfection. It is true that in one sense Christ's perfection—His righteousness—meets all our needs. In that sense, He is "THE LORD OUR RIGHTEOUSNESS."[13]

But in another sense there is a degree of perfection which those who are saved must have developed before Christ comes. "We often hear it said that it is what Jesus has done for us, and not anything that we can do for ourselves, that will secure for us heaven. This may be true in one sense, but in another it is not true. There is a work for us to do to fit ourselves for the society of angels. We must be like Jesus, free from the defilement of sin. . . . We have a work to do to fashion the character after the divine model. All wrong habits must be given up."[14] We "must engage in the warfare against sin and Satan, or [we] will fail of [attaining] everlasting life."[15]

That perfection which God demands of us—and which He makes attainable to us—is not absolute perfection, but that perfection of character which results from growth in Christ. It is a perfection which results from the proper exercise of the will—that kingly power which God has given each of us to develop characters patterned after Him.

If this were not true—if there were no battles to be fought, no temptations to be resisted, no victories to be gained, no characters to be developed, no perfection to be reached—why would God admonish us to "resist the devil"?[16] Why would He tell us to "fight the good fight of faith,"[17] and to "put on the whole armour of God"?[18]

But there *are* battles to be fought and won; there *are* victories to be gained; there *is* a character to be developed. For "the Lord requires perfection from His redeemed family." He calls, not for absolute perfection, but "for perfection in character-building."[19]

Although we will have a *sinful nature* as long as we are living on the battlefield of this earth, we can and must develop a *sinless character.* This is the "perfection in character-building" which God requires and which He makes possible for each one of us. Through the indwelling of Jesus Christ, we may develop characters which resemble—but do not duplicate—the character of God. "By faith in Christ and obedience to the law of God we may be sanctified, and thus obtain a fitness for the society of holy angels and the white-robed redeemed ones in the kingdom of glory."[20]

But first we must be "saints upon the earth."[21]

---

1. SC 23
2. Hebrews 6:6
3. GC 489 (emphasis supplied)
4. 4T 355
5. John 15:5
6. TM 456
7. See DA 429; RH, Aug. 28, 1894; ST, April 15, 1913
8. DA 311 (emphasis supplied)
9. RH, March 10, 1904 (emphasis supplied)
10. OHC 278
11. Series A, No. 1, Second Edition, November 1890, page 45
12. Matthew 5:48
13. Jeremiah 23:6
14. RH, Nov. 17, 1885
15. OHC 218; RH, June 20, 1882
16. James 4:7
17. 1 Timothy 6:12
18. Ephesians 6:11
19. 5 BC 1085
20. SL 83
21. TM 145

# Chapter 9
# You Can Be More Than a Match for Satan

The war between Christ and Satan has been going on now for approximately six thousand years. But instead of becoming less severe with the passing of time, it has increased in intensity so that the battle is being fought more sharply today than at any other time in history.[1]

### Violence in the World
As Satan's time grows shorter and he becomes more desperate, he resorts to every device and tool and method that his evil mind can think of. Thus violence has become an increasingly useful tool in his hands.

We can see the enemy's work in the headlines of almost any daily newspaper. In front of me just now is a copy of what is probably a typical newspaper.[2] Notice the headlines from this one issue:

"Dupont Plaza Hotel Fire: 96 people killed."

"Train Wreck Kills 14: 175 Others Injured in Amtrack's Worst Accident Ever."

"Quake Shakes Aleutian Islands."

"Bank Failures Most in 1986 Since '30's"

"Year Sees 41 Children Shot to Death in Detroit."

"Homeless Man Burns to Death."

"Pipe Gets Blame for Alpine Blast Which Killed 7 People."

And so read the headlines, day after day, telling their story of crime, violence, and destruction. Is it any wonder that one demonic voice said during a spiritual battle, "Being kind is not my nature. My nature is to kill and destroy"? Violence and destruction, both by man and by the forces of nature, will become more frequent and severe as the great controversy reaches its final stages.

The enemy uses his tools of violence and destruction on the largest scale by inciting wars. He delights in war, for it excites the worst of human passions and then sweeps its victims to their eternal death by thousands and millions. War also diverts the minds of many people from preparing to meet their God.[3] War and rebellion, which originated in the mind of Satan, are so much in harmony with his character and purpose that they have become some of his most useful tools.

### Bewitchment in the Church

But, as we would expect, the tools Satan uses in conducting his war on the church are different from those he uses in the world. He knows very well how to adapt his weapons to his "enemy"—God's redeemed children. In the church, Satan uses a much more subtle approach. Paul alluded to this when he asked, "O foolish Galatians, who hath bewitched you, that ye should not obey the truth?"[4] In making war with the church, Satan more often than not casts a bewitching spell over the followers of Christ, so subtle, so soothing, so hypnotic in effect, that his victims are not aware of what is taking place.

Satan casts this bewitching spell over every church member whose mind is not directly under the influence of the Holy Spirit, and then he can mold those minds as he chooses.[5] Thus it is that every one of us is every day controlled by one or the other of the two contending powers.[6] "Every man, woman, and child that is not under the control of the Spirit of God is under the influence of Satan's sorcery."[7]

In chapter 5 we discussed some of the more common ways in which many professed Christians tempt Satan to tempt them. They dare Satan to tempt them, and he always accepts the challenge. Most of those with whom I have prayed in spiritual warfare can point to some experience in their lives in which they opened the door to Satan. They invited the enemy in, and he accepted the invitation, as he always does. But Satan cannot touch the mind or intellect unless we yield it to him in some way.[8]

## Satan and the Unborn

As shocking as the thought may be, the truth is Satan can work upon an unborn child through the influence of the parents. Demonic influence can be exerted upon a fetus at the time of conception and passed on from generation to generation.

Do you remember the account of the father who brought his demon-possessed son to Christ for healing at the foot of the mount of transfiguration? Jesus asked the father, "How long is it ago since this came unto him? And he said, Of a child."[9] I doubt if Jesus asked that question for His own information. He already knew the answer. But He wanted us to know that Satan can possess children as well as adults. And that influence can begin before the child is born.

God visits "the iniquity of the fathers upon the children unto the third and fourth generation."[10] But, you say, that isn't fair. Of course it isn't fair! Sin is never fair. It is not fair that every human being born into this world since the fall of Adam and Eve has had to pay a price for their mistake. But that is the nature of sin. It is not fair that a child should be born with a physical or mental handicap, but it happens. Why are we so naive as to think that children are not born with *spiritual* handicaps?

Several years ago I baptized a young woman who was then confined to a wheelchair. Since then she has become confined to her hospital bed, where she has lain for six years, unable to move any part of her body except her head and a slight movement of one arm. Because of her affliction, she has been unable to speak for the past two years. She is the mother of three young children. She is still young; she recently celebrated her thirty-fourth birthday. Life has not been "fair" to this young woman.

I remember an older woman whom I baptized a few years

ago. She, too, was confined to a bed. Both of her feet had been amputated. She was almost totally blind and almost completely paralyzed. Satan had succeeded in bruising her body severely, but he could not destroy her soul. She is sleeping now, awaiting the return of the Life-giver, whom she learned to love. Life was not fair to her, either.

I do not profess to know any more than you do all the reasons why God permits such things to happen. But if these cases serve no other purpose, they remind us that we are living on a battlefield, where the war is just as real as the casualties are.

Life on a battlefield is never pleasant. Perhaps these casualties serve not only to remind us of the reality of the war, but also to prevent our becoming too attached to this world. Perhaps God allows these things to happen so that we will look forward with longing to the time when "God shall wipe away all tears. . . ; and there shall be no more death, neither sorrow, nor crying,"[11] when "the eyes of the blind shall be opened, and the ears of the deaf shall be unstopped. Then shall the lame man leap as an hart, and the tongue of the dumb sing."[12]

In the meantime, we see war casualties all around us. They are in our homes, in our churches, in our schools, in our hospitals, and on the streets of our cities. Some of them are members of our own families. They are victims of disease; of physical, emotional, and sexual abuse; of broken homes and divorce. Some of them are casualties because of their own choice of lifestyle, but they are casualties nevertheless. And children are often the victims of choices in which they had no voice. It is not fair, but it is one of the realities of a very real war.

And it is one of the realities of the war—whether we choose to believe it or not—that satanic influences can be transmitted from one generation to another. I can recall a number of cases in which I have been asked to do spiritual battle for three generations of the same family, all of whom had serious demonic problems. Passing his control from one generation to the next is one of Satan's devices of which we can remain ignorant only at great risk.

## How People Become Possessed

For most of us, the real battle begins when we are confronted with a temptation. The length and severity of the battle will depend largely upon the extent to which Christ controls the mind. When Satan confronted Jesus, he found no response. Later, Jesus could truthfully say, "The prince of this world cometh, and hath nothing in me."[13]

As it was with Jesus, so it may be with us. In our conflict with Satan, we may "have all the help that He had."[14] The battle can be short because Jesus—who has already won the war—is so completely in control of our minds and wills that nothing in us responds to the temptation. So it was with Joseph when Satan tempted him through Mrs. Potiphar.

Sometimes the battle is short for another reason. Too often the battle is only a small skirmish because we give in to the enemy without a struggle. We capitulate to Satan.

But when in Christ's strength we successfully resist one temptation, it becomes easier to resist the next temptation, even though it may be in a different area of human experience. That is because when we resist Satan, we turn a little of our wills—that kingly power which God has given to us—over to the control of the Holy Spirit, and our wills are strengthened. "Every temptation resisted, every trial bravely borne, gives us a new experience, and advances us in the work of character building."[15]

But the opposite is also true. When we give in to the enemy and yield to the temptation, we "short-circuit" the Holy Spirit. *We weaken our power to resist the enemy.* We make it easier to yield to the next temptation, either in the same area of human experience or in another. In this way, we open the door to Satan; we invite him to tempt us again. "Every act of transgression reacts upon the sinner, works in him a change of character, and makes it more easy for him to transgress again. By choosing to sin, men separate themselves from God, cut themselves off from the channel of blessing, and the sure result is ruin and death."[16]

*Every time we intentionally and knowingly yield to Satan's suggestion, we turn a little of our wills over to him. In this way* our wills gradually become weakened. As our wills and power of resistance become weaker, we may eventually lose the ability even to *choose* to resist Satan. When this condition exists in one area of our lives, it becomes easier for that same experience to be repeated in other areas. *To the extent that this condition exists in a person's life, that person is controlled or possessed by Satan.*

I do not know of any line that distinguishes between extreme control and possession. If there is one, it's very thin.

### Lack of Control

"I am not in control" is the most common comment made by those who come for spiritual battle. Lack of control is the common thread that runs through the experience of these people. This lack of control can involve any phase of human experience, but there are four areas in which the enemy finds us especially vulnerable. The scope of this book will allow only a very brief discussion of each area.

1. *The spiritual life.* Satan knows very well that anyone whom he can influence to neglect prayer and Bible study will eventually be overcome by his attacks. Therefore, he will do anything he can to prevent our reading the Bible, praying, attending religious services, or engaging in any activity which will strengthen a relationship with the Saviour. One of his most successful approaches is to keep us so occupied with *good* things that we don't take time for the *essential* things. "Sabbath sickness" is very real with many of these people. It is not coincidental that people with physical problems seem to get worse on Friday evenings or Sabbath. The enemy will do anything he can to prevent our being exposed to the truths of God's Word.

2. *The disposition.* "I can no longer control my temper" is a statement often made by those who seek deliverance from demonic control. Demonic voices often identify themselves as *Anger, Temper, Hate, Resentment, Jealousy, Pride* (as in Donna's case), *Selfishness,* and *Impatience.*

3. *Appetite.* Demons whose assignment it is to pervert the appetite are among the most frequently encountered in the

deliverance ministry. "Satan is constantly on the alert to bring the [human] race fully under his control. *His strongest hold on man is through the appetite,* and this he seeks to stimulate in every possible way."[17]

Appetite will be the ruin of thousands of professing Christians. If they would but conquer on this point, they could gain the victory over all other temptations.[18] We can be sure that as we draw closer to the end, Satan's temptations in the area of appetite will become more powerful and more difficult to overcome. Many victories must yet be gained on this point before Jesus comes.

4. *The sex life.* This is an especially sensitive area because it involves so many aspects of our being. Our physical bodies, especially the nervous system, our moral, spiritual, and emotional natures—all are involved in the sex life. Satan knows how vulnerable we are in this area, and he takes full advantage of his knowledge and of our weakness.

Because we are so vulnerable in this area, Satan often uses it as an entering wedge; and once he gains control in this area, it is easy for him to extend his influence into other areas until, in many cases he controls the entire life. The downfall of the demoniac of Capernaum began with his practice of masturbation.[19] Troops commonly serving under the Demon of Sex are Masturbation, Sexual Fantasy, Lust, Adultery, Fornication, and Homosexuality.

The enemy "adapts his temptations to all classes" of people—the educated and the illiterate, the youthful and the aged, the rich and the poor.[20] No class of people and no individual is immune from Satan's attacks apart from Jesus Christ. Satan is seeking an entrance into your life, your home, and your family right now. That's his business in this war.

## You Can Be More Than a Match

But there is good news! In spite of Satan's power and perseverance, *not one of us needs to be defeated.* Jesus Christ, our Creator and the Son of God, left heaven and came down to the battlefield and defeated the enemy on his own "turf." It is true that we have a powerful enemy;[21] but in Jesus we have a more powerful ally—One who has "all power. . . in heaven and in earth."[22] More than that, "a guardian angel is appointed to every follower of Christ. These heavenly watchers shield the righteous from the power of the wicked one."[23] How important it is that we not walk on Satan's ground where the angels will not go, and leave them behind!

One of the most encouraging statements about the great controversy is this one: "Through divine strength the *weakest saint* is more than a match for him [Satan] and all his angels."[24] I like that! I am one of the "weakest saints," and I need all the help I can get. How about you?

That "divine strength" comes only from the presence of Jesus Christ in the heart, but that presence is available to everyone. "Behold," He says, "I stand at the door and knock: if any man hear my voice, and open the door, I will come in to him, and will sup with him, and he with me."[25] He is waiting now. Why not invite Him in, even if you have invited Him in before?

If that invitation is extended sincerely, He will come in. And He will begin at once to bring about the needed changes in your life. "By His perfect obedience He has made it possible for every human being to obey God's commandments. When we submit ourselves to Christ, the heart is united with His heart, the will is merged with His will, and the mind becomes one with His mind, the thoughts are brought into captivity to Him; we live His life. This is what it means to be clothed with the garment of His righteousness."[26]

There is no other way to win the war—but we *can* win! "Thanks be to God, which giveth us the victory through our Lord Jesus Christ."[27]

---

1. UL 20
2. *The Jackson* (Tennessee) *Sun,* Monday, January 5, 1987.
3. GC 589
4. Galatians 3:1
5. MCP 22
6. 5T 102

7. MYP 278
8. MS 17, 1893
9. Mark 9:21
10. Exodus 20:5
11. Revelation 21:4
12. Isaiah 35:5, 6
13. John 14:30
14. 9T 22
15. ST, Feb. 5, 1902; RC 349
16. Letter 96, 1896; 6BC 1058
17. CD 150 (emphasis supplied)
18. CD 163
19. DA 255-257; MH 91-93
20. GC 600
21. SC 122
22. Matthew 28:18
23. GC 512, 513
24. 5T 293 (emphasis supplied)
25. Revelation 3:20
26. COL 312
27. 1 Corinthians 15:57

# Epilogue

## Questions Commonly Asked About Spiritual Warfare

**Q:** *How do you see spiritual warfare or the deliverance ministry in view of the counsel Mrs. White gave in the Mackin case?*

**A:** Space does not permit a lengthy discussion of the Mackin case, which you can read about in *Selected Messages,* book 3, pages 363-378 and elsewhere in Mrs. White's writings.

A careful reading of the Mackin case reveals the following facts: (1) The Mackins "spoke in tongues." (2) They believed that Mrs. Mackin had received the gift of prophecy. (3) They "declared" people to be possessed by demons and then *pretended* to cast them out. (4) They acted in a dramatic way, "as if you were on a stage." (5) They had conducted themselves at camp meeting and elsewhere in such a way as to create a disturbance.

Mrs. White's disapproval of their work was based on the five factors listed above rather than on the fact that they were involved in spiritual warfare in a legitimate way.

If we conclude that Mrs. White opposed the casting out of demons *per se,* we must also conclude that she was inconsistent with *her own* writings, for she wrote that "souls possessed with evil spirits will present themselves before us. We must cultivate the spirit of earnest prayer, mingled with genuine faith to save them from ruin, and this will confirm our faith. God designs that the sick, the unfortunate, *those possessed with evil spirits shall hear his voice through us.*"[1]

If we conclude that Mrs. White opposed the casting out of

demons, we must also conclude that she was inconsistent with her own *work*, for she herself rebuked demons, as attested to by her own words: "Satan takes possession of the minds of men today. In my labors in the cause of God, *I have again and again met those who have been thus possessed, and in the name of the Lord I have rebuked the evil spirit.*"[2]

Mrs. White and her husband on a number of occasions did spiritual battle on behalf of themselves and members of their family, as we have recounted in chapter 3.

There is nothing in the Mackin story to discourage spiritual warfare if it is done properly and in harmony with Scripture.

**Q:** *Why does it take so long for some people to be delivered? In Christ's day deliverance seems to have been instantaneous.*

**A:** I do not have a simple answer to this question; but if we put several ideas together, we may arrive at what may at least be a partial answer.

In the first place, I am not sure that all of the deliverances done by the Saviour were instantaneous. Take, for example, the case of Mary Magdalene "out of whom went seven devils."[3] The Bible gives no information other than what is contained in that one clause. But Mrs. White revealed, "Seven times she [Mary] had heard His rebuke of the demons that controlled her heart and mind. She had heard His strong cries to the Father in her behalf."[4] No matter how we may choose to interpret this statement, it is apparent that the deliverance was not completed by the first of Christ's commands or rebukes. Mary's deliverance must therefore have consumed some time, and in that sense it was not instantaneous. Mary's deliverance required more than one command from the Saviour.

We usually think of the deliverance of the demoniac of Gadara, recorded in Mark 5:1-19, as being instantaneous. The King James Version leaves the impression that Jesus commanded the evil spirits to leave, and they all left immediately in response to that one command.

But the original language gives a different concept. Let us look at verse 9. In the Greek, the verb *asked* is in the imperfect action form, which indicates an ongoing or repeated action, as "kept on asking" or "continued to ask." On the other hand, the verb *answered* is in the aorist form, which indicates an action which takes place only once and is not repeated. Although the King James Version does not give that rendition, some other versions do. *An Expanded Translation,* for example, reads, "And he kept on questioning him, What is thy name?" *Young's Literal Translation* says, "And he kept questioning him, What is thy name?"

In the same way, the King James Version gives the impression that Jesus commanded one time that the demons come out, and they all responded to that one command. However, many other well-recognized translations give a different wording. The Douay Version, for example, says, "He was saying to him, 'Go out of this man, thou unclean spirit.' " The New English Bible reads, "Jesus was already saying to him, 'Out, unclean spirit, come out of this man!' " And the New American Standard Bible says, Jesus "had been saying to him, 'Come out of the man you unclean spirit.' "

In these versions and in others,[5] the command of Jesus is presented as an ongoing or repeated action. It was not a matter of Jesus giving one command and all the demons responding to that one command, as we usually picture it. The deliverance of the demoniac of Gadara consumed some time.

There are still other factors to be considered relative to the time consumed in deliverance. These spiritual battles are as real as any battle fought between the armies of nations.[6] But battles do take time, even spiritual battles. Therefore we should not be surprised that victories do not come instantaneously. Also to be considered is the fact that Satan is a hundred times more powerful than he was when he rebelled in heaven,[7] and ten times more powerful than he was in the days of the apostles.[8] It is still true that Jesus has "all power"; but since Satan leaves only when forced to do so, and since he has more power with which to resist, this may be a factor in the time consumed.

I suspect that the most important human factor is the yielding of the will. It is not easy for some people to surrender their wills to another—even to Jesus Christ. I know of some cases in which several days passed while those persons wrestled with that problem. Satan sees to it that the surrendering of the will to Jesus under those conditions is not easy.

It was this matter of surrendering the will that delayed the victory and prolonged the battle in the case of Cyrus.[9] That battle went on for *three weeks,* and even then, Jesus Himself had to bring His influence to bear upon Cyrus before the satanic powers could be overcome. "For three weeks Gabriel wrestled with the powers of darkness, seeking to counteract the influence at work on the mind of Cyrus; and before the contest closed, Christ Himself came to Gabriel's aid."[10] Why should we question or doubt the validity of spiritual warfare when the battle goes on for *three hours?*

Putting all this information together, and having witnessed the changes for good that spiritual warfare and the deliverance ministry make in human lives when the battle has ended, I am not troubled by the fact that deliverance in some cases takes a few hours.

**Q:** *Isn't there danger in "parleying with the enemy" during spiritual battle? Haven't we been warned not to do this?*

**A:** There is risk involved whenever we are confronted by the enemy, whether it is in spiritual battle or in a "simple temptation." There is always the possibility of yielding to the enemy. We are never safe from his influence without God's protection.

Yes, we are cautioned against "parleying with the enemy." "By parleying with the enemy, we give him an advantage."[11] "It is unsafe to enter into controversy or to parley with him [Satan]."[12] But we are also told that there are times when we must acknowledge the fact that we are sinners and must *tell the enemy* that 'Christ Jesus came into the world to save sinners.' "[13]

There are times during deliverance sessions when it is necessary to "tell the enemy." Ruth had allowed herself to be hypnotized many times. During the spiritual battle, a demon of hypnotism said, "I don't have to leave her. She has allowed herself to be hypnotized many times. She invited me in, and she is mine."

I replied, "Yes, Ruth did that, and it was a sin. But she has confessed that sin, and it has been covered with the blood of Jesus Christ. You now have no legal right to hold that sin against her. In the name of Jesus Christ whom Ruth and I choose to serve, I demand that you leave her."

The same situation arose when we were praying for Charles, who, although he had been reared in an Adventist home, had come to a situation in his life where he had prayed to Satan. Again the demon refused to leave, claiming that Charles's praying to Satan gave him grounds for staying. Again I rebuked the demon in the name of Jesus, acknowledging that Charles was indeed a sinner, but that his sin was covered with the blood of Jesus. I did this because in both cases Satan's attack was so severe at that time that both Ruth and Charles were unable to speak. And in both cases, the demons had to flee, as they always do when confronted in spiritual battle with the name of Jesus.

We must never parley with the enemy in the sense of conversing with him, arguing with him, or seeking information from him. But there are times when we must "tell the enemy." There are times when we must "make a charge upon the enemy when required of God to do so."[14] Mrs. White writes about those who have "no courage to contend for the right, to venture something in the warfare, and to learn how to attack Satan and take his strongholds. . . . Somebody must venture; someone must run risks in this cause."[15]

**Q:** *Do all who experience a deliverance stay free?*

**A:** Deliverance frees those who were formerly oppressed from Satan's *domination,* but not from *temptation.* We can be sure that Satan renews his attacks on former captives with greater intensity than ever, and some have been recaptured. That is another sad reality of the war.

Jesus taught that it was possible for those who have been delivered to be reinfested with evil spirits. "When the unclean spirit is gone out of a man, he walketh through dry places, seeking rest; and finding none, he saith, I will return unto my house whence I came out. And when he cometh, he findeth it swept and garnished. Then goeth he, and taketh to him seven other spirits more wicked than himself; and they enter in, and dwell there: and the last state of that man is worse than the first."[16]

Only when we recognize the subtle and destructive nature of Satan's power over human minds and the terrible contaminating influence he exercises over those whom he dominates, can we begin to realize the extreme difficulty of remaining free from that power once he has possessed them.

Few people—even among us Seventh-day Adventists—realize the deadly nature of sin and of Satan's power as it really is. "When men and women fall under the corrupting power of Satan, it is *almost impossible* to recover them out of the horrible snare so that they will ever again have pure thoughts and clear conceptions of God's requirements. Sin, to their deluded minds, has been sanctified by the minister, and it is never again regarded in the loathsome light that God looks upon it. After the moral standard has been lowered in the minds of men, their judgment becomes perverted, and they look upon sin as righteousness, and righteousness as sin."[17]

If these words tell us anything at all, it is that our only safe course is to avoid Satan's snares at all costs. Not one of us can safely play with Satan's toys, walk on his ground, tempt him in any way, or yield even to the smallest of his temptations. To do any of these things is to risk contamination by the deadly poison of Satanic influence, for which Jesus Christ is the only antidote. But the hypnotic, mind-altering effects of Satan's presence puts the victim at great risk, not because God lacks power to heal, but because the victim may have sacrificed his power to realize his need or to make that choice.

To stay free after one is delivered, he or she must put on a full suit of spiritual armor every day.[18] This is the only way to keep from becoming Satan's captive in the first place.

The fact that a few who were once freed become reenslaved does not in any way invalidate spiritual warfare or the deliverance ministry. *We do not close hospitals because some patients die in them!* According to Scripture and the writings of Mrs. White, spiritual warfare and the deliverance ministry will be valid as long as the gospel commission is in force.[19]

**Q:** *Is it possible for a person to cast demons out of himself, or to "deliver himself," so to speak?*

**A:** We must recognize that no one is ever delivered by any power other than that of Jesus Christ. Without Him, we can do nothing.[20] In that sense, the answer to this question must be No. In that sense, no one can cast out devils. But Jesus "called unto him his twelve disciples, [and] gave them power against unclean spirits, to cast them out, and to heal all manner of sickness and all manner of disease."[21] Even Judas, who was himself possessed by demons of greed and selfishness, was empowered by the Saviour to rebuke demons and cast them out just as the other eleven disciples were. It is in that sense—through power originating in Jesus Christ, but channeled through the human agent—that anyone can do any of God's work. In that sense, a truly surrendered Christian can engage in spiritual battle by praying on his own behalf and asking God to rebuke any satanic forces in him, in the same way that he would pray an intercessory prayer for anyone else.

In one of his letters to Timothy, Paul suggests that Timothy instruct "those that oppose themselves; if God peradventure will give them repentance to the acknowledging of the truth; and *that they may recover themselves out of the snare of the devil,* who are taken captive by him at his will."[22] I would suggest that spiritual warfare is involved in the daily putting on of the armor.

It is important to know, however, that *it is not always possible for people to do spiritual warfare on their own behalf.* People—even professing Christians—may find themselves in situations where it is impossible for them to free themselves from Satan's snares. Mrs. White writes about those who have become so deeply entrapped by Satan that they cannot free themselves. It is this type of problem I have been involved with in my experience in the deliverance ministry.

Mrs. White writes about individuals who must "entreat those who have had a religious experience, and who have faith in the promises of God, *to plead with the mighty Deliverer in their behalf."* Even then, she says, "It will be a close conflict."[23] It is difficult to realize how severe and how close the conflicts can be until you have witnessed some of them.

The same author writes about "those who depart from the right and venture upon his [Satan's] ground." Of these she says, "When they wish to control themselves they cannot. They yielded their minds to Satan, and he will not release his claims, but holds them captive. No power can deliver the ensnared soul but the power of God *in answer to the earnest prayers of His faithful followers."* [24]

In every church there should be a group of "His faithful followers" who would hold up before the Lord in spiritual battle those who are being oppressed by the enemy, those who are sick or discouraged. If every church had such a group praying and interceding for unconverted relatives and friends, and for the outpouring of the Holy Spirit, what a power for God and for good it would exert. This is a ministry in which every Christian can engage. This would be in harmony with God's counsel that we pray "always with all prayer and supplication in the Spirit, and watching thereunto with all perseverance and supplication for all saints."[25]

**Q:** *Why does the deliverance ministry have to be so spectacular?*

**A:** After having witnessed literally hundreds of spiritual battles, I can tell you that there is very little that is dramatic or spectacular about them. Yes, in some cases demonic voices do speak out. But I must tell you that the most spectacular thing about spiritual warfare or the deliverance ministry is the spectacular changes it makes in the lives of those who have been delivered from Satan's power.

*And what is wrong with the spectacular?* Many of the events which happened in the Old Testament, as well as in the New Testament, were no doubt spectacular. The crossing of the Red Sea, the giving of the Ten Commandments at Sinai, the fall of Jericho—these and many other events in which God was in charge must have been very dramatic. God deals with the dramatic and spectacular. Certainly the raising of the widow's son at Nain (see Luke 7:11-16), Jairus's daughter (see Luke 8:41-56), and Lazarus (see John 11:40-45), and the many miracles of healing performed by Jesus were considered dramatic and spectacular by those who witnessed them. How can we believe otherwise?

God has told us that we are to see wonderful manifestations of His power before Jesus comes. Let us thank God that the time has come. The war is almost over!

"There is to be in the churches a wonderful manifestation of the power of God, but it will not move upon those who have not humbled themselves before the Lord, and opened the door of the heart by confession and repentance. In the manifestations of that power which lightens the earth with the glory of God, they will see only something which in their blindness they think dangerous, something which will arouse their fears, and they will brace themselves to resist it. Because the Lord does not work according to their ideas  and expectations, they will oppose the work. 'Why,' they say, 'should not we know the Spirit of God, when we have been in the work so many years?'—Because they did not respond to the warnings, the entreaties of the messages of God, but persistently said, 'I am rich, and increased with goods, and have need of nothing."[26]

May God help each of us to be humble and to keep open the door of our hearts by confession and repentance, so that having been victorious warriors with Jesus in battle, we may also be partakers with Him in glory.[27]

---

1. MS 65B, 1898 (emphasis supplied)
2. 2SM 353 (emphasis supplied)
3. Luke 8:2
4. DA 568
5. See Today's English Version and The New American Bible
6. MB 119
7. 3T 328
8. 2SG 277
9. Daniel 10:12, 13
10. PK 572

11. DA 121
12. 3T 483
13. SC 36 (emphasis supplied)
14. 3T 316
15. 3T 316
16. Luke 11:24-26
17. 5T 143 (emphasis supplied)
18. Ephesians 6:11-18
19. Matthew 10:1, 8; Luke 9:1; Mark 16:15-18; DA 823, 350, 351; EW 227; MS 176, 1898
20. John 15:5
21. Matthew 10:1
22. 2 Timothy 2:25, 26 (emphasis supplied)
23. 1T 344 (emphasis supplied)
24. 1T 299 (emphasis supplied)
25. Ephesians 6:18
26. RH Dec. 23, 1890
27. SDG 156

We'd love to have you download our catalog of
titles we publish at:

www.TEACHServices.com

or write or email us your thoughts,
reactions, or criticism about this
or any other book we publish at:

TEACH Services, Inc.
254 Donovan Road
Brushton, NY 12916

info@TEACHServices.com

or you may call us at:

518/358-3494

Produced in partnership with
LNFBooks.com